Praise for *The Republican Workers Party*

The spirit of Buckley's endeavor represents what is finest in the Trump moment, and what is best in conservatism, too.

—Daniel McCarthy, *American Conservative*

An early and confident Trump supporter, Buckley makes a persuasive argument that Trump has reshaped American politics, opening up opportunities for ordinary people which his predecessors blocked off.

—Michael Barone, co-author, *The Almanac of American Politics*

The best explanation of Trumpism that I've seen.

—Marvin Olasky, *The World*

Buckley is by turns scathing, funny, and sympathetic, but always well-informed. He rolls the stone away from the American heart.

—Allen Guelzo

An important and provocative book.

—Michael Ledeen, *Front Page Magazine*

Frank Buckley is one of the most astute observers of the modern American scene.

— Deroy Murdock

Praise for *The Republic of Virtue*

Bracing stuff . . . his writing is lucid and often witty.

—*Wall Street Journal*

Political corruption, in the form of crony capitalism, is a silent killer of our economy. Frank Buckley's new book shows how we can rein it in and help restore the Republic.

—William Bennett, former Secretary of Education

This is Buckley at his colorful, muckraking best—an intelligent, powerful, but depressing argument laced with humor.

—Gordon S. Wood, Pulitzer Prize winner

Praise for *The Way Back:*
Restoring the Promise of America

Frank Buckley marshals tremendous data and insight in a compelling study.

—Francis Fukuyama

Best book of the year.

—Michael Anton

Praise for *The Once and Future King:*
The Rise of Crown Government in America

His prose explodes with energy.

—James Ceasar

THE LOOMING THREAT
OF A NATIONAL BREAKUP

American
Secession

F.H. BUCKLEY

New York • London

First American edition published in 2020 by Encounter Books,
an activity of Encounter for Culture and Education, Inc.,
a nonprofit, tax exempt corporation.
Encounter Books website address: www.encounterbooks.com

Manufactured in the United States and printed on
acid-free paper. The paper used in this publication meets
the minimum requirements of ANSI/NISO Z39.48–1992
(R 1997) (*Permanence of Paper*).

FIRST AMERICAN EDITION

LIBRARY OF CONGRESS CATALOGING-IN-PUBLICATION DATA
Names: Buckley, F. H. (Francis H.), 1948– author.
Title: American secession : the looming threat of a national breakup /
by F. H. Buckley.
Description: New York : Encounter Books, [2020] |
Includes bibliographical references and index.
Identifiers: LCCN 2019018857 (print) | LCCN 2019981176 (ebook) |
ISBN 9781641770804 (hardcover) | ISBN 9781641770811 (ebook)
Subjects: LCSH: Secession—United States. | Polarization (Social
sciences)—United States. | States' rights (American politics) |
United States—Politics and government—21st century. |
United States—Politics and government—Philosophy.
Classification: LCC JK311 .B83 2020 (print) |
LCC JK311 (ebook) | DDC 320.973—dc23
LC record available at https://lccn.loc.gov/2019018857
LC ebook record available at https://lccn.loc.gov/2019981176

For Esther, Sarah, Nick and Benjamin Herbert

CONTENTS

PREFACE

This is a book about breakups, about how countries split apart and how the United States is ripe for secession. Across the world, established states have divided in two or are staring down secession movements. Great Britain became a wee bit less great with Irish independence, and now the Scots seem to be rethinking the 1707 Act of Union. Czechoslovakia is no more and the former Soviet Union is just that: former. Go down the list and there are secession groups in nearly every country. And are we to think that, almost alone in the world, we're immune from this?

Countries threaten to split apart when their people seem hopelessly divided. I've seen it already. Before moving to the United States, I lived in a country just as divided, without the kind of fellow feeling required to hold people together. Canada was an admirably liberal country, and yet it came within a hair's breadth of secession. America is headed the same direction today, and without the reserve and innate conservatism that has permitted Canadians to shrug off differences.

We're less united today than we've been at any time since the Civil War, divided by politics, religion and culture. In all the ways that matter, save for the naked force of the law, we are already divided into two nations just as much as in 1861.The contempt for opponents, the Twitter mobs, online shaming and no-platforming, the growing tolerance of violence—it all suggests we'd be happier in separate countries.

That's enough to make secession seem attractive. But there's a second reason why secession beckons. We're overlarge, one of the biggest and most populous countries in the world. Smaller countries, as I'll show, are happier and less corrupt. They're less inclined to throw their weight around militarily, and they're freer. If there are advantages to bigness, the costs exceed the benefits. Bigness is badness.

It might therefore seem odd that we've stayed together so long. If divorces are made in Heaven, as Oscar Wilde remarked, how did we luck out? The answer, of course, is the Civil War. The example of Secession 1.0 in 1861, with its 750,000 wartime deaths, has made Secession 2.0 seem too painful to consider. But this book will explode the comforting belief that it couldn't happen again. The barriers to a breakup are far lower than most people would think, and if the voters in a state were determined to leave the Union they could probably do so.

To begin with, we're far more likely to let it happen today than we were in 1861. John Kerry had a point when he said that Putin, by invading Crimea, was behaving as if it were the nineteenth century. While the secretary of state was mocked for what seemed like naiveté, public attitudes have in fact changed since 1861. We are now less willing to take up arms in order to maintain the Union and readier to accept a breakup instead.

Second, a cordial divorce might be worked out through the amending machinery of a convention held under Article V of the Constitution, if all sections of America were good and tired of each other. Secession cannot be unconstitutional when there's a constitutional way of making it happen, through a constitutional convention.

Finally, the Supreme Court might revisit its denial of a right of secession. The originalists on the Court would recognize that the Framers had thought that states had the right to secede, while the more politically minded members of the Court might hesitate before ruling secession illegal and permitting the president to make war against a state. Instead, the Court could be expected to look northward, to the more nuanced view of secession rights taken by the Canadian Supreme Court, which rejected both an absolute right and an absolute bar to secession.

So it's not difficult to imagine an American breakup. The reasons why a state might want to secede today are more compelling than at any time in recent history. Slavery isn't on the ballot, and there would be no undoing of the civil rights revolution anywhere. Indeed, the states with the most active secession movements are progressive and want to escape from a federal government they think too conservative. Were secession to happen today, it would be politically correct.

So it might happen. I see us on a train, bound for a breakup. The switches that might stop us have failed, and if we want to remain united we must learn how to slow the engine. That will take things that have been in short supply lately: a greater tolerance for ideological differences, thicker skin to imagined slights, a deeper repository of confidence in and sympathy for our fellow Americans. These are things we used to have, and can learn to have again if we recognize that the alternative is secession.

Federalism used to allow for greater differences among the states, and that permitted us to sort out our differences by settling among people with like beliefs. And while federalism was discredited when it sought to excuse racist Jim Crow laws in the South, we've left that world long behind. That is why I propose, as a solution to our divisions and an antidote to secession, a devolution of power to the states—not mere federalism, but the alternative that the British presented to the Continental Congress in 1778 after it had decided upon secession through the Declaration of Independence. It was what Gladstone and Charles Stuart Parnell sought as an alternative to Ireland's outright secession. The solution was "home rule," and if adopted in America this would return more power to a seceding state than it possesses now, or ever possessed under American federalism.

Part I will examine the case for a breakup as a solution to our deep social and political divisions. Split into two countries, we'd probably get along better with each other, and there are feasible ways in which this might happen. Part II will then look at secession as a cure for bigness. Smaller countries are happier, less corrupt, and better governed, and we're one of the biggest countries around. Finally, Part III will discuss alternatives to outright secession, for while that's a distinct possibility, this book is meant as a call to civility and a warning to those who seek to divide us. Before you criminalize honest policy differences, before you dox your ideological enemies and drive them from restaurants, remember that they have exit options!

PART I

~

A CURE FOR A DIVIDED PEOPLE?

We've hit rock bottom.

—Senator John Kennedy (R-LA)

1

ONE NATION, DIVISIBLE

Meet Don Livingston. He's a South Carolina native who taught philosophy at Emory University. A respected academic, he's the author of two well-regarded books on David Hume and "an exceptional presence in Hume studies" according to a reviewer in a leading philosophical journal.[1] He is courtly, ironic and bearded, the very picture of an academic philosopher. He's also a secessionist.

Livingston isn't just a secessionist, mind you. He's also a southern partisan. The first time I met him, in Montreal, he was sporting Stars and Bars suspenders and wanted to talk about the Quebec independence movement. In 2003 he founded the Abbeville Institute, named after the birthplace of John C. Calhoun in South Carolina. The Abbeville Institute explores "what is true and valuable in the Southern tradition," its writers, customs and songs. The institute hosts a summer school for college and graduate students on the constitutional right of secession and on all the things that are wrong with Massachusetts.

It's easy to dismiss all this as cranky tomfoolery. Since the Civil War, the idea of secession has been consigned to the political loony bin. But that's about to change, and not just in the South. Among philosophers, secession is increasingly respectable.[2] Before long, we'll hear our politicians take it up too.

The Eternal South

Because of the Civil War, we see secession through the prism of differences between the North and the South, and especially the original sin of American slavery. After the war, slavery was abolished and the Union was preserved. And yet the South has always been different, and always will be. It's an indigestible part of the Union, with traditions and institutions unlike those of the rest of the country. Southerners are more likely to serve in the military, as Robert E. Lee Prewitt did in *From Here to Eternity*. Their accent is different, the food is different, the music is different and the manners are very different. They'll smile at strangers and tip their hats to ladies. When their mothers ask if they want a piece of pie, they'll say "Yes, Ma'am." And if you thank them, they're apt to say "You're welcome," not merely "un-huh."

For southern whites, every home is Tara and every ancestor a Confederate general and the descendant of laughing cavaliers, in a prelapsarian past they cling to all the more fiercely because it is so irretrievably lost. They must live with the knowledge that they, alone among Americans, are a defeated people and have been justifiably scorned for the institution of slavery before the Civil War and their treatment of African Americans thereafter. What that has given their best fiction writers is a darkness and sense of guilt called Southern Gothic.

In Flannery O'Connor's *Everything That Rises Must Converge*, a recent college graduate lives in a decayed southern town with his mother, who embarrasses him with her absurd family pride, her racism and her boundless love for him. One day a black woman, outraged by the mother's condescension, strikes at her and she collapses on the sidewalk. Her son lectures her contemptuously on her need to come to terms with the new racial realities, but the blow will kill her and she dies of a stroke. Her racism is unconscious, while his supercilious liberalism is conscious, heartless and inexcusable. Both are self-deceived and live in a fallen world of inescapable sin. Compare this with the rest of American literature, where go-ahead individuals get ahead, where justice triumphs over evil and tragedy is unknown, and it's hard to imagine anything more foreign to northern sensibilities than Southern Gothic.

That distinctiveness has made a literary and sociological genre out of southern culture, as described by writers such as Edmund Wilson and James Cobb.[3] It has also given us the delicious satire of Florence King, with her tales of bubbas and good old boys, of Scarletts and Melanies.[4] From the North, Chuck Thompson hilariously describes everything that's wrong about southerners and concludes we'd be better off without 'em.[5] Back in 1860, James Pettigru famously described his own state of South Carolina as too small for a republic and too large for an insane asylum.

Since Pettigru's time, the South has steadily grown in population, as people have moved there from other parts of the country. Now there are urban pockets that don't look anything like the surrounding counties. Voters in my own city of Alexandria, Virginia, are very progressive, as are voters in Austin, Texas, and in North Carolina's Research Triangle. And can anyone explain Florida to me?

Northerners call this the New South, and diehard southerners call it the "No South." At the same time, southern culture has migrated to the heartland. The NASCAR circuit, which began in Daytona Beach and Charlotte, with ex-bootleggers from the Thunder Roads of Tennessee and North Carolina, now has racetracks in Illinois and Arizona. As for southern music, it's gone global. There are jazz clubs in Russia, country and western radio stations in Sweden, rock groups everywhere. We're all a little southern now, waiting on the levee for the Robert E. Lee.

Nevertheless, the South is still distinctive, after all these years. A recent study of how people feel about Don Livingston's Stars and Bars flag or Confederate military heroes reveals that many southerners, particularly conservatives and Protestants, still embrace their southern identity.[6] For liberals in the North too, the South remains another country, a darker one. It's the place where three civil rights workers were murdered in 1964, the land of the White Citizens Councils and Senator Jim Eastland (D-MS). It's where people cling to their guns and religion, as Barack Obama said. It's the place you brand as alien in order to feel good about yourself.

So the differences remain. Even when not at war, North and South have been divided and this has led to three different compacts between them. The first, beginning with our founding and continuing to the Civil War, tolerated slavery as a legal matter. That ended with the war and Reconstruction, and a second compact followed, which suppressed the rights of African Americans and lasted until the civil rights revolution of the 1960s. The third compact brought an anomalous period of good feelings, which seems now to have ended, and with it the willingness to tolerate any differences between the North and the South.

In the first compact, the country accepted southern slavery at the 1787 Philadelphia Convention which gave us our Constitution, and thereafter lived with it until the Thirteenth Amendment abolished it in 1865. Before the Civil War, slavery was well protected. Fugitive Slave laws permitted slaveowners to seek out and capture escaped slaves in the North, and the Supreme Court in its *Dred Scott* decision held that Congress could not ban slavery in any of the territories. Even if emancipated, an African American descendant of slaves could never become a U.S. citizen, the Court ruled.[7] As James Buchanan reminded the southerners in 1860, if all that they wanted was to preserve slavery, they had no reason to secede.

The second compact began with the end of Reconstruction in 1876, and lasted until the 1960s. Slavery was abolished, but the former Confederate states were permitted to suppress black votes, enact Jim Crow laws and even tolerate lynchings. In 1912, the country overlooked Woodrow Wilson's racism to elect him president. He had been the president of Princeton and the governor of New Jersey, but he never forgot his southern roots. His *History of the American People* cast a honeyed eye on slavery: far from being Simon Legrees, most slaveowners were kind and humane men, he wrote, and "domestic slaves were treated with affection and indulgence, cared for by the mistress of the household."[8] Once in office as president, he promptly resegregated the civil service.

What southerners called the War of Northern Aggression was never forgotten. In the Spanish-American War, a Rough Rider who had been a Confederate officer saw the Spaniards retreat and called out, "Let's go, boys! We've got the damn Yankees on the run again!" Still, northerners and southerners made a conscious decision to mend the wounds of war, an effort in which Robert E. Lee took a leading part. Two months after the surrender he applied to the U.S. government for a pardon, and then asked his fellow southerners to abandon their animosities and come to terms with their defeat. He wrote to a magazine editor that "it should be the object of all to avoid controversy, to allay passion, give full scope to reason and to every kindly feeling."[9]

Lee's endeavor to reconcile southerners with the North was greatly appreciated, and he became a national hero. President Grant invited him to the White House in 1869. President Eisenhower said that he admired Lee extravagantly and hung a portrait of him in his office.[10] Lee was depicted on four U.S. postage stamps, and *The Dukes of Hazzard* remembered him with the General Lee muscle car. Writing in 1962, Edmund Wilson saw Lee as America's last eighteenth-century hero: "The classical antique virtue, at once aristocratic and republican, had become a national legend, and its late incarnation in Lee was to command a certain awed admiration among Northerners as well as Southerners."[11]

The effort at reconciliation was an enormous success. When the veterans of the Army of Northern Virginia and the Army of the Potomac reenacted Pickett's Charge on its fiftieth anniversary in 1913, they met at the crest of Cemetery Ridge, clasped hands and buried their faces in each other's shoulders. The next morning, President Wilson said to the veterans, "we have found one another again as brothers and comrades,...enemies no longer, generous friends rather."[12] Had any doubt remained, the Pledge of Allegiance that children recited each morning at school affirmed that we were "one nation, indivisible." Some southerners invited people to say "one nation, *divisible*," but that never caught on.

All this happened at the same time that the country struggled with the task of assimilation, of making Americans out of the millions of immigrants who flocked to our shores. Generations of Irish, Italian and eastern European children were taught of our country's heroes and recited the Pledge of Allegiance at school. Bing Crosby treated Protestants to a look at an all-American Catholic school run by Sister Ingrid Bergman in *The Bells of St. Mary's*, and Christians laughed at Marx Brothers comedies and whistled the songs of Irving Berlin. But one group was left behind and relegated to second-class status, and that was African Americans. There was a tradeoff for the reconciliation between the North and white southerners, and it was the abandonment of Reconstruction and the goal of racial justice.

The second compact came to an end in the 1960s, with the outrage over the murder of civil rights workers, the 1964 Civil Rights Act, the 1965 Voting Rights Act and the enforcement of the Supreme Court decision of *Brown v. Board of Education*. A generation of Americans came of age seeing pictures of police dogs attacking protesters and of U.S. marshals escorting little black girls to school. Then the South abandoned its Jim Crow laws and looked much less racist, or at least not much more racist than the North. While southern states had suppressed African American votes in the 1960s, fifty years later things had completely turned around. In places like Alabama and Mississippi, black turnout now exceeded white turnout and minority candidates held office in record numbers.[13] The Great Migration of African Americans northward had ended, and their children were returning to the South.

In the third compact, state-sponsored forms of discrimination were banned, but expressions of southern pride would be tolerated. The historian Shelby Foote called it the Great Compromise. Southerners would admit that it was good that the Union had won, while northerners would concede that the Confederates had fought bravely. The Sons of Confederate Veterans could hold their marches, the reenactors could gather at the old campground, the Confederate statues would stay up. If one had to specify a date when this compact began, it was 1969, the year that Bob Dylan released *Nashville Skyline* and The Band sang "The Night They Drove Old Dixie Down." Back then the singers were the unacknowledged legislators of mankind. It was the year that Nixon became president.

When the Ken Burns documentary on the Civil War aired in 1990, it was so generous to the Confederacy that Burns felt obliged to tell viewers that he was happy the North won. In 1995, George F. Will offered an affectionate look at a southerner's unreconstructed adherence to an antimodern culture and the goofball secessionist movement of Don Livingston and his friends.[14] As recently as 2015, the *Washington Post* ran stories commemorating the sesquicentennial of the Civil War, paying tribute to both sides. From their defeat, white southerners were permitted to retain some measure of dignity in the memory of their battlefield heroes.

But now the third compact has ended. The Confederate statues are coming down, the Stars and Bars flag is a provocation and expressions of white southern pride are deemed racist. In Alexandria, Virginia, Christ Church took down the portrait of Robert E. Lee, and for good measure that of slaveholder George Washington. Both had worshipped at the church, and Washington had helped pay for it. The highly partisan Southern Poverty Law Center links Don Livingston to racism, saying that while he purports to study secession from a philosophical perspective, it all comes down to a defense of the slaveholding antebellum South. Philosophical or not, southern secessionists are presumed to be acting in bad faith.

That doesn't sound anything like the Don Livingston I know, notwithstanding those suspenders. He's the gentlest of people, and quite without a trace of racism. But what about his defense of a right of secession? Constitutionally, it might look like a dead letter ever since Lee's surrender at Appomattox in 1865. All the same, the demise of the third compact is going to fray the sense of national unity that has stilled secessionist sentiments. If millions of people in one section of the country are told that they're presumptively evil, and that the presumption really can't be rebutted, they're going to wonder if they belong somewhere else. "Some of those folks—they are irredeemable, but thankfully they are not America," said Hillary Clinton. Yet if they're not Americans, they might reasonably ask themselves to what country they belong, or should belong.

The Crack-Up

Some northerners would be just as happy to see the South become another country. Here's one of them, the *New Yorker*'s Dan Piepenbring, writing in 2018 about his visit to Chick-fil-A, a southern chain restaurant that is expanding into New York. For Piepenbring, this was an "infiltration." The headquarters of the Atlanta-based restaurant "are adorned with Bible verses and a statue of Jesus washing a disciple's feet," and what made the dining experience "especially distasteful" was the "commercial-evangelical messaging…infected with this suburban piety."[15] The article reeks with scorn, but Piepenbring was simply telling us what the Deep North thinks about southerners.

It's gotten much worse since the 2016 election, and now the divisions are broader than North versus South. Today it's liberals versus conservatives and especially progressives versus Trump supporters. At an awards dinner, the actor and Presidential Medal of Freedom winner Robert DeNiro brought a Hollywood crowd to their feet with cries of "F___ Trump!" Then there's Kathy Griffin, who held up a bloody head of a decapitated Trump. And Stephen Colbert, whose *Late Show* put Stephen Miller's head on a spike. And Madonna, who said, "I've thought a lot about blowing up the White House." When even Mick Jagger worries about the polarization and lack of civility, you know it's serious.

It's not just Hollywood. When Trump separated children from their parents at the border, the normally level-headed Joe Scarborough said, "I don't want little children ripped from their parents' arms. I don't want them marched off to showers." Michael Hayden, former CIA director, tweeted that "other governments have separated mothers and children," and he added a photo of Auschwitz.[16] The respected *Foreign Policy* magazine published an article saying that, for the first time in America's history, a Nazi sympathizer occupied the Oval Office.[17] Violence has been normalized, and when Rand Paul (R-KY) was attacked by a neighbor, and suffered six broken ribs, lung damage and multiple bouts of pneumonia, Kasie Hunt laughingly said on MSNBC that this was one of her "favorite stories."

The extremism has gone mainstream, and the oracles of respectable liberalism now embrace the vilest of left-wing extremists. Sarah Jeong tweets "it's kind of sick how much joy I get out of being cruel to old white men," and is rewarded with a position on the *New York Times* editorial board. For its part, the *Washington Post* sends little billets-doux to Antifa thugs.[18] They cover their faces and beat up conservatives, but Minnesota's progressive attorney general, Keith Ellison, has endorsed the Antifa handbook, and CNN's Don Lemon said in their defense that "no organization is perfect."

News reporters no longer pretend to hide their biases, and stories about their opponents are supercharged with snarling adverbs, witless sarcasm and heartless derision. In the past, that would have gotten a reporter fired, but no longer. Today, radicalism is profitable and pays for itself through higher subscription rates from partisan readers who feast on their hatreds.[19]

Trump has accused congressional Democrats of treason, and they have repaid him with interest. After Trump met with Vladimir Putin at a summit in Helsinki, Chuck Schumer (D-NY), the Senate minority leader, speculated that the Russians had blackmailed Trump, and Steny Hoyer (D-MD), the House minority whip, accused Trump of treason.[20] Senator Ed Markey (D-MA) canceled meetings with Brett Kavanaugh after his nomination to the Supreme Court on the grounds that he had been nominated by an "illegitimate" president. Markey isn't the sharpest knife in the drawer, and may not have realized that the military would therefore be excused from obeying Trump's orders as commander in chief if that were so. Or perhaps Markey *had* thought of that. After all, Representative Steve Cohen (D-TN) tweeted that the military should mount a coup, as they do from time to time in South America.

And why the heck not, if conservatives are the irredeemably deplorable people that Hillary Clinton said they are? If Trump is Hitler, as the *Washington Post* suggests,[21] then you're a collaborator unless you join the resistance, with more than words too. At a minimum, there's no need to talk to anyone on the other side.

We thought it couldn't get any crazier, but the political divide and the breakdown in trust became even deeper after Kavanaugh's confirmation hearings. When Anita Hill accused Clarence Thomas of sexual harassment in 1992, we were permitted to disagree about who was telling the truth. No longer. On the left, fury has been weaponized and moral outrage has supplanted political debate. Hillary Clinton told her supporters, "You cannot be civil," while Eric Holder, the former attorney general, chided Michelle Obama's niceness: "Michelle always says, 'when they go low, we go high.' No. No. When they go low, we kick them."[22] We've hit rock bottom, with no clear path up.

Before the 2016 election, Trump said he might not accept its results. Clinton said this was horrifying and that it cast doubt on our institutions. But when he was elected, she didn't hesitate to join the "Resistance" herself, and what has followed is nothing more than the working out of that movement's grim logic. It's brought us to a crisis of the house divided, like the one to which Lincoln referred in his debate with Stephen Douglas. If anything, we were a more united country before the Civil War. At Harvard College, Henry Adams could befriend Robert E. Lee's son, who within a few years would become Major General Rooney Lee, C.S.A. You'll not find much of that today between liberals and any Trump supporters, at Harvard or elsewhere.

And what happens next? When our opinion leaders tell us that we're a hair's breadth away from fascism, that's how a civil war begins. And is that impossible to imagine? A poll in 2018 found that 31 percent of likely voters think there will be a another civil war within the next five years.[23] In that light, secession looks attractive to many of us. Another poll around the same time found that a full 39 percent of Americans wanted to secede from America, including 42 percent of Democrats.[24]

FIGURE 1 COUNTY-LEVEL VOTING, 2016 ELECTION

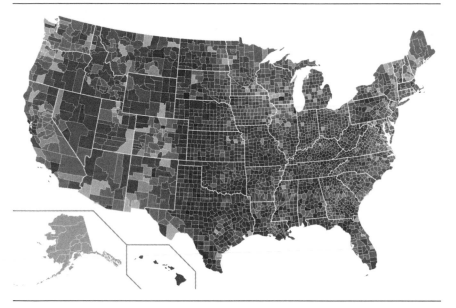

As Figure 1 illustrates, we've cleaved apart in our voting patterns, with bicoastal Democrats at the country's edges and a Republican heartland in between.[25] Looking at the map, it's not hard to see how two or three countries might emerge from a split. And is that so improbable? Many in the North, including Lincoln, thought secession quite unlikely in 1860.[26] There wasn't a solid South, and there was strong unionist sentiment in Virginia, North Carolina and Tennessee.[27] Robert E. Lee was a unionist, as was Stonewall Jackson, until their state seceded. Alexander Stephens, the Confederate vice president, was also a unionist until Georgia seceded. Many of the border states that remained in the Union were equally divided. And yet secession happened. All it took was a South Carolina to get the ball rolling, and the same would be true today.

We might not even need Fort Sumter this time. Social media might do the trick, as it did during the Arab Spring of 2011. We're already dividing ourselves online. Check your Facebook friends, and ask yourself how many of them disagree with your politics. A Pew study reports that two-thirds of conservatives and half of liberals say that most of their close friends share their political views. There's a good chance we'll unfriend those who don't: 44 percent of liberals and 31 percent of conservatives say they've dropped Facebook friends over politics.[28]

The two political parties increasingly campaign as if we're two separate countries. With their identity politics, the Democrats have become the intersectional party of racial and sexual minorities, of immigrants and feminists. On the right, the battle lines are drawn and the *Wall Street Journal* editorializes that "we're all deplorables now."[29] For his part, Trump didn't bother to campaign in liberal states such as California.

We've come to resemble the divided Canada that Lord Durham visited in 1838. He had expected to encounter political differences, but what he discovered was "two nations warring in the bosom of a single state." It's the same for the United States today. In our politics, we're already two nations.

A Constitutional Crisis

There's been a revival of nationalism among conservatives, but this hasn't served to unite the country. When liberals equate conservative nationalism with racism, that doesn't help. In addition, conservative nationalists themselves have a flawed understanding of American nationalism, one that isn't grounded in the nation's history and traditions.

The icons of American nationhood are the liberal principles expressed in the Declaration of Independence and guaranteed by the Bill of Rights. Other countries have their common cultures or religions. What America has is an idea that constitutes our identity as Americans, and that idea is liberalism in the classical sense. American nationalism therefore is necessarily liberal nationalism. If we are to resist the call to secession, it is our allegiance to our country's liberal principles that will unite us.

Conservative nationalists don't buy this, however. Some of them explicitly reject America's liberal traditions, seeing them as charged with secret Enlightenment codes that dissolve all they hold dear. Classical liberalism, they say, has drowned the most heavenly ecstasies of religious fervor and chivalrous enthusiasm in the icy water of egotistical calculation. To quote *The Communist Manifesto*. But in their dismissal of the Founders' principles, illiberal conservatives throw away the only set of ideas that could unite us. An antiliberal American nationalism is therefore self-defeating.

Other conservative nationalists say they're not illiberal, they don't reject the foundational principles of liberty, but they argue that nationalism must be based on something more than an idea. They dismiss what's called "creedal nationalism" as insufficient. We're more than a creed, the say. We're also a community with a common set of values and beliefs about how to advance the common good. We're the kind of country that Samuel Huntington described in *Who Are We? The Challenges to America's National Identity* (2004), a country that is British and Protestant in origin. But if we were ever that, we're certainly not that today, and those common values, beliefs and affections have been replaced by gridlock, rancor and *deux nations*. For this reason, the conservative nationalist should be a secessionist. He tells you he loves America. It's just other Americans he hates.

Sadly, it's becoming less and less likely that the liberal principles of the Constitution could unite us. When Justice Kavanaugh was confirmed, the liberal columnist E. J. Dionne wrote that the Supreme Court's legitimacy is in tatters.[30] The president nominated Kavanaugh, as the Constitution requires, but many liberals think Trump an illegitimate president because more people voted for Clinton. As for the Senate, which voted to confirm Kavanaugh, it's illegitimate too because little North Dakota has the same number of senators as California. If all three branches of government are illegitimate, however, the fault lies deeper than any individual. It's the Constitution itself that is at fault.

In truth, the Constitution is partly to blame for our crisis. With its separation of powers, it requires the assent of the president and the two houses of Congress before legislation is passed. For over two hundred years this worked well, as people on either side met in the middle to agree on the bills that needed passing. Shared ideals and a common patriotism drew people together for the good of the country, and as much legislation was enacted in periods of divided government as when one party controlled both houses of Congress and the presidency.[31]

That ended in 2010, when the Affordable Care Act was passed without a single Republican vote in the House or the Senate. Republican amendments were rejected by a stern Obama, who told them that "elections have consequences" and reminded them, "I won." A month later, however, another election gave control of Congress to the Tea Party Republicans, and thereafter gridlock was the order of the day. The separation of powers, with the need for president, Senate and House ordinarily to agree on legislation, was supposed to prevent bad laws from being enacted. But inevitably bad laws are enacted and then prove impossible to repeal. And all of this is made worse by the absurd (and imaginary) requirement of a sixty-vote majority in the Senate to overcome a filibuster.

What that's given us is a constitutional crisis, our second since the Civil War. In 1861, our Constitution proved incapable of resolving the differences among us. Now too, on health care, immigration reform and so many of the issues that divide us, stasis reigns and necessity is met with impossibility. Our Constitution has been justly admired, but it was made for a citizenry very different from the angry Americans of today. And, as in 1861, that's a recipe for secession.

2

WHEN SECESSION IS POLITICALLY CORRECT

I f our Constitution has failed us, if we're so divided, secession wouldn't seem far away. That's simply the logic of the right of national self-determination proclaimed in Woodrow Wilson's Fourteen Points.[1] If the Austro-Hungarian Empire was overlarge and too diverse, then break it up, said Wilson. That gave the world four new countries, including Czechoslovakia and Yugoslavia, and when they were found to be overlarge they broke into a total of nine different countries.

There's at least as strong a case, on theories of national self-determination, for a breakup of the United States. We're overlarge, and we've sacrificed the trust and fellow feeling that a common national identity used to provide. We've become poorer and less caring for those reasons, and that makes secessionism look progressive and nationalistic.

Progressive Nationalism

Nationalism promotes trust, which the philosopher Jon Elster calls the cement of society.[2] I'll find it easier to reach an agreement with people I trust and to rely on their promises. I'll not expect them to welch on their commitments or opportunistically try to renegotiate their promises down the road when they have a threat advantage. And I'll rely on

17

them to carry out the promises that courts could never enforce. I will take their side and will not betray them. That's why trusting societies are wealthier ones,[3] and why we might be richer after a breakup if that made us more trusting.

Nationalism also promotes solidarity, the sense of attachment to and sympathy with others that is one of the most basic of human goods. It will pull one leftward on economics, since it asks one to support social welfare programs for fellow citizens. Not aliens, mind you. The nationalist will distinguish between aliens and citizens, but what he would deny the former must be paid for by what he would give the latter. Otherwise the pose of nationalism is a pious fraud. That's why libertarians who object to social safety nets cannot be nationalists.

We sacrifice the wealth gains of trust and the sense of solidarity when we're so divided among ourselves. The number of people who trust the federal government all or most of the time has fallen from 77 percent in 1964 to 19 percent in 2015.[4] We don't feel much better about our fellow citizens either. Only a third of Americans say that most people can be trusted, down from half in 1972.[5]

If that's where we are now, imagine what it would be like in an easily imaginable future America, where Trump has won reelection and a Democratic House of Representatives has impeached him. Suppose further that Ruth Bader Ginsburg has gone the way of all flesh and a dispirited Stephen Breyer has resigned, giving Trump two more seats on the Supreme Court, which he fills with religious conservatives. From prominent Democrats, there are daily calls for resistance in the streets, and our restaurants and theaters have turned into no-go zones for people of the wrong political party.

This argues for secession, as a cure for our social ills. If we split apart, we'd be more likely to find ourselves living with people whom we trust and with whom we share bonds of solidarity. We'd be more prosperous, since we'd find it easier to rely on people to keep their promises, and we'd be more willing to look after each other with generous social welfare programs. In that sense, nationalism is progressive.

Progressive Secessionism

It's not 1860, and secession movements are different today. They're politically correct. Let's look at the Yes California independence campaign, led by Marcus Ruiz Evans. It's calling for a "Calexit," echoing Brexit, and the movement has been gathering steam ever since Trump was sworn into office and started abandoning all manner of progressive causes. He has withdrawn America from the Paris Climate Accords and wants to open the California coast to offshore drilling. He has throttled back Obama's auto emission standards and plans to revoke California's right to set its own standards. To add insult to injury, he has slapped a 30 percent tariff on imported solar panels.

From its headquarters in "Fresno, Republic of California," Yes California makes the financial case for secession. In 2016 the state paid $103 billion more in federal taxes than it received back from Washington. The Yes California pitch to the state's voters even sounds a bit like Trump, railing against foreigners, but in this case they're people in other states: "California loses billions of dollars every year supporting states whose people hate us and our culture. Let's keep our taxes in California and invest in our people first." In effect, says Yes California, the state is being invaded by foreigners, "just like the armies of Rome and England occupied and controlled and extracted resources from Europe and India."

Yes California is soliciting signatures for a "self-determination" ballot measure that would ask California voters whether the state should become independent. If it passed, it would lead to another referendum, which if passed would require the state legislature to issue a formal declaration of independence. An independent California would then have the world's fifth largest economy, with a population greater than Poland, Canada or Australia. It's an awesome state already, says Yes California, and it would be even more incredible if it were an independent country. Someday soon, you might need a passport before you could bring the kids to Disneyland.

It might happen. California is just different. It has always been different, and that used to be something the rest of the country admired. It was the land of the *Beverly Hillbillies*, swimmin' pools, movie stars. But now it's the state that bans offers of plastic drinking straws while giving heroin users free hypodermic needles. California has become the symbol of utopian excess, and a place where conservatives wouldn't want to live.

But California isn't alone when it comes to talk of secession. There's also a proposal for a new country of Cascadia, comprising the states of Oregon and Washington plus the Canadian province of British Columbia. It would be home to sixteen million people in the emerging megaregion that stretches from Vancouver to Portland, and would unite people with the same kinds of ideas about the environment, Starbucks and yoga.

That would take two secessions, of course, one from the United States and the other from Canada, followed by a union. And what would that new country look like? Would it be a republic, like Washington and Oregon, or a monarchy, like British Columbia, celebrating its link to Great Britain over high tea at the Empress Hotel in Victoria? The proposed national anthem of "O Cascadia" does seem inspired by "O Canada." Sample lyrics:

Rich grows the wealth when balance and integrity
Can cultivate good health and foster industry to be
Diverse as your people, O Cascadia,
Capable and just, purposeful and green.

The Cascadia Independence Party still has to sort out the details: where Queen Elizabeth fits in, how to accommodate the First Nations, and so on. It isn't certain about the borders, and dreams of a Greater Cascadia that would include Idaho, Montana and Alaska. But it assures us that Cascadia will be dynamic and inclusive, with "bio-regional awareness." The rest of the mission statement is a work in progress.

If that all sounds a little grandiose, the secessionist movement in Vermont can at least look back to a time when the state was independent. It seceded from Britain in 1777 and took its time joining the United States. It played off Canada and the Continental Congress for better terms, and only joined the United States in 1791. Not even Texas was independent for a longer period of time.

Vermont isn't much like the rest of the country. It's rural but liberal, and it sends Bernie Sanders and Patrick Leahy to Washington. It's the least religious state in the country, and also the whitest. The Vermont secession movement gathered steam when George W. Bush was president. In 2004, Kirkpatrick Sale drafted a "Middlebury Declaration" that was positively anti-American. "The national government has shown itself to be clumsy, unresponsive, and unaccountable," it said. Imagine how the Vermont secessionists feel about the national government now.

Over in the land of Calexit, Trump's withdrawal from Obama-era environmental mandates makes Marcus Ruiz Evans hopping mad. Don Livingston of South Carolina, on the other hand, bemoans women in the military and same-sex marriage. Ruiz Evans and Livingston are like the partners in an impossible marriage. It doesn't matter who's right when the differences are irreconcilable. And both might be right. Perhaps California and South Carolina shouldn't be in the same country. Ruiz Evans doesn't want to live in a country that includes South Carolina, and Livingston doesn't want to live in a country that includes California. They're not rivals so much as allies.

It gets harder and harder to think that separatism is intrinsically suspect when it's a worldwide phenomenon supported by people from every ideological perspective.[6] On the right, there's the New Flemish Alliance, which wants Flanders to secede from French-speaking Wallonia in southern Belgium. On the left, there's the Parti Québécois, which wants Quebec to secede from the rest of Canada. There are moderately conservative Catalan separatists in Spain and moderately left-wing Scottish separatists in Great Britain. Secession is often accomplished without violence, as happened on the amical breakup of Czechoslovakia into Slovakia and the Czech Republic. But sometimes it takes a war, as happened in the case of Yugoslavia, and in the American secession from Britain in 1776. If you think that breakups are always bad, do you regret the American Revolution?[7]

When secession begins to look mainstream, even progressive, we might have to reconsider our rankings of presidents, elevating James Buchanan and perhaps taking Abraham Lincoln down a notch or two. If a California secession referendum were to pass, would we really want another Lincoln to suspend the writ of habeas corpus and send in an invading army? Even if there were a southern Secession 2.0? It would be nothing like Secession 1.0, since no one is defending slavery, and 70 percent of today's Americans were born after the Selma civil rights marches. Secession was once the most retrograde of causes, but now it's politically correct. So let's consider how we might go about it and whether it could ever succeed.

3

SECESSION:
A HOW-TO GUIDE

Secession. It's a crazy idea, right? But it's less crazy than you might think. With all the secessionist movements across the world, it becomes easier to imagine breakups, even in the United States. It's easier still when the pluses are so much greater than they were in the past, and the minuses so much smaller.

The pluses are much greater today because the federal government's footprint has grown so much larger. In the past, the states had less reason to chafe at rule from Washington. A spring in the back yard didn't become a federal wetland. Teachers didn't receive letters from the Department of Education telling them how to run their schools. Local highway decisions weren't made in Washington because of the strings attached to federal grants. Now America increasingly looks more like a unitary state than like the federal republic the Framers of the Constitution thought they had given us. With secession, we would reverse course.

If there's more reason for a state to secede today, there's also a much smaller downside. It wouldn't perpetuate slavery in the South, as secession in 1861 would have done. Even after the Civil War had brought an end to slavery, federalism and "states' rights" were discredited by southern Jim Crow laws and barriers to voting registration for black Americans. Since then, however, the civil rights revolution has taken hold and it's much less likely that secession would be employed to discriminate against a minority. Even notorious racists such as Senator Jim Eastland (D-MS) understood how the 1965 Voting Rights Act and federal marshals had changed the equation. "When [the blacks] get the vote," he said, "I won't be talking this way anymore."[1] Far from bringing back Jim Crow, secession today, such as a Calexit, might give us the perfect paradise of woke progressivism.

Instead of the Civil War, think of the "velvet divorce" of the Czechs and the Slovaks in 1993. Distinct in religion, language and culture, they had been combined in a country created in 1918 after the collapse of the Austro-Hungarian Empire. The Slovaks were conservative and agricultural while the Czechs liked avant-garde plays and rock music. Czechoslovakia suffered through Nazi and Soviet rule, and then split apart into Slovakia and the Czech Republic upon the fall of communism. The two new countries, both Western and liberal, solved questions about their border, the division of assets and assumption of public debt through negotiation, and they've since maintained the friendliest of relations.

We're now living in a secessionist moment in world history, as a result of three international developments. The first was the decolonization movement, which gave birth to new countries in Africa and Asia as European empires shrank. Like the American Revolution, the grant of independence was a form of secession from the colonial power. The second development was the end of the Cold War. When countries had faced the threat of Communist expansion, they did not wish to weaken themselves by dividing in two, or weren't given that option. South Vietnam wasn't permitted to remain independent of North Vietnam, for example. But after the Communist empire fell, twenty-four new countries emerged from behind the Iron Curtain.[2] The third development was a worldwide embrace of free trade. When countries subjected foreign goods to high tariffs but let domestic goods pass freely, small size meant greater barriers to trade, and that was a cost. If a seceding state could enter into a free-trade zone with the one it was splitting away from, and accede to its free-trade treaties, that cost would disappear.

All this points to a probable rise in American secessionism. To American states that chafe at rule from Washington, the federal government can seem like a distant and burdensome colonial power. That was the point of the Tea Party movement, after all. "Party like it's 1773!" said Sarah Palin, recalling the first Tea Party. The fall of communism has also lessened the need for the powerful military that only a large state can provide. Finally, a seceding state might hope to retain free-trade links with the rest of the United States, as Quebec separatists had sought with their idea of sovereignty-association.

In short, the stakes have been lowered, and that's why a modern president might react to a secession referendum with more of James Buchanan's prudence and less of Abraham Lincoln's unyielding assertion of federal sovereignty. Secession might also seem like a reasonable way to resolve unbridgeable partisan differences, in which case an Article V convention to amend the Constitution might work out our own velvet divorce. Finally, the right of secession might find support in the Supreme Court, were it to follow the decision of the Canadian Supreme Court when it was faced with the possibility of a successful independence referendum in Quebec.

Cass Sunstein has said that "no serious scholar or politician now argues that a right to secede exists under American constitutional law."[3] He's right. But I will show how it could still happen through constitutional means.

Rehabilitating James Buchanan

President James Buchanan (1857–61), pompous and dithering, was wholly incapable of solving the secession crisis. An ardent defender of slavery, he seems to have had a hand in crafting the Supreme Court's notorious *Dred Scott* decision. As president, he managed to infuriate northern Democrats and the Republican abolitionists without winning over southern secessionists. Historians routinely list him as the worst of our presidents.

But what do they know? It's all too easy to fall prey to the hindsight bias when judging past actions. We know just how the coach blew the Sunday football game—on Monday morning. We know the pitcher should have been pulled—but only after he had given up the home run. So try to imagine yourself in Buchanan's shoes before the Civil War began, and ask yourself what you would have done.

Buchanan delivered his fourth and last State of the Union address on December 3, 1860. The harvests had been abundant, the factories were booming, and plenty smiled upon the entire country, he said. "In short, no nation in the tide of time has ever presented a spectacle of greater material prosperity than we have done until within a very recent period." Two weeks later, delegates to a South Carolinian secession convention voted unanimously to leave the Union. It was what everyone had expected, and Buchanan puzzled over why this should be so.

He blamed abolitionists like William Lloyd Garrison. Their "long-continued and intemperate" opposition to slavery had led to unnecessary sectional differences, Buchanan said in his address. Inspired by "vague notions of freedom," southern slaves were encouraged to revolt, and slaveowners had begun to fear servile insurrections. But there was no need for secession, he insisted. If the point was to defend slavery, no country better protected it. In *Dred Scott*, the Supreme Court had upheld the slaveowner's property rights in his slaves, even in the western territories, and the Fugitive Slave laws had made it illegal to assist runaway slaves who had fled north for their freedom.

Buchanan conceded that Abraham Lincoln, the president-elect, was no friend of slavery. But Lincoln had received less than 40 percent of the popular vote, with four parties contending for the presidency in 1860. He would have to govern as a constitutional president, under a Constitution that protected slavery. Indeed, Lincoln would begin his first inaugural address by telling southerners, "I have no purpose, directly or indirectly, to interfere with the institution of slavery in the States where it exists. I believe I have no lawful right to do so, and I have no inclination to do so."

Still, southerners didn't like Lincoln. But that didn't give them the right to secede, Buchanan said. Southerners were mistaking the federal government for a voluntary association that could be dissolved at pleasure by any state. But it wasn't. If it were, the Union would be "a rope of sand, to be penetrated and dissolved by the first adverse wave of public opinion in any of the States."

And so the southern states had neither a reason nor a right to secede. But what was a president to do when they did leave the Union? Was he to make war on them? As Buchanan reminded us, the

Framers didn't think so. They debated the question when they considered Madison's proposal for a new constitution in his "Virginia Plan." Article 6 of the plan would have granted the federal government the right to disallow unconstitutional state laws, and further provided that Congress might "call forth the force of the Union" against any state that failed to fulfill its duties. But when the latter provision came up for discussion at the Constitutional Convention in 1787, Madison regretted it, and said, "The use of force against a state, would look more like a declaration of war, than an infliction of punishment, and would probably be considered by the party attacked as a dissolution of all previous compacts by which it might be bound." Madison proposed that this provision be tabled, and his motion passed unanimously.[4] Then, a few days later, he returned to the impossibility of sending federal troops to coerce a state: "Any Govt. for the U. States formed on the supposed practicality of using force agst. the (unconstitutional proceedings) of the States, wd. prove as visionary & fallacious as [government under the Articles of Confederation]."[5]

The question of employing force against a state arose again when the delegates debated Article IV, Section 4, clause 2, which provides that the United States "shall protect each [state] against invasion; and on application of the legislature, or of the executive (when the legislature cannot be convened) against domestic violence." From their debates, it is clear that the only kind of invasion the delegates had in mind was one by a foreign country.[6] And Lincoln agreed, before the war began. "Would the marching of an army into South Carolina...without the consent of her people, and in hostility against them, be coercion or invasion?" he asked. "I very frankly say, I think it would be invasion."[7]

But when Alexandria, Virginia, was invaded on May 24, 1861, it was the federal government that sent in the troops.

Leaving constitutional questions aside, what about the political decision that Buchanan faced? He didn't want a civil war, and in 1860 most Americans agreed with him. Like Lincoln, many Americans thought that the South was bluffing and would come to its senses in its own good time. But if not, a war was clearly to be avoided. From Herald Square, the mass-circulation *New York Herald* editorialized that "the citizens of the free states are not prepared for civil war, nor will they consent to imbue their hands in the blood of their brethren at the South."[8] In the rival *New York Tribune*, Horace Greeley agreed. If seven or eight states wanted to leave the Union, "we shall feel constrained by our Devotion to Human Liberty to say, Let them go!"[9] Abolitionists in particular would have been happy to see the South leave, and thus to rid the country of the scourge of slavery. In fact, William Lloyd Garrison had proposed a national disunion convention to expel the South, and had burned a copy of the U.S. Constitution after invoking the prophet Isaiah and calling it "a covenant with death, and an agreement with hell."[10]

If people in 1860 preferred disunion to war, they would have been still less inclined to fight had they known that the war would kill 750,000 people—a sum higher than the total from all other American wars before and since.[11] When the southerners bombed Fort Sumter in Charleston Harbor in April 1861, they thought they were simply working out the logic of secession. But the attack enraged the North and gave Lincoln a justification for calling up 75,000 volunteers to retake the federal forts. That in turn prompted Virginia and North Carolina to join the other southern states in secession. It is not too much to say that America blundered into the Civil War, as foolishly as the countries of Europe when they awoke to find themselves at war in 1914.

And the war came. So Lincoln said in his second inaugural address, as though it were a natural disaster that could not have been avoided. Thereafter he prosecuted it with unstinted determination, which of course is the only way to fight a war. He also assumed near-dictatorial powers to imprison and silence those who opposed him, under the plea of necessity.

When Lincoln took office, Washington, D.C., was cut off from the North by the slave state of Maryland, which might have seceded if he hadn't imprisoned several of its politicians. One of them was John Merryman, who had helped destroy several bridges to prevent federal troops from reaching the beleaguered federal capital. Ever since Magna Carta, the writ of habeas corpus has been a citizen's chief defense against arbitrary arrest and detention, and Chief Justice Roger B. Taney issued the writ to free Merryman. In response, Lincoln purported to suspend the writ. Taney then ruled in *Ex p. Merryman* that Lincoln lacked the authority to do so, because only Congress could suspend the writ.[12]

Lincoln loathed Taney because of the Supreme Court's decision in *Dred Scott*. Ward Hill Lamon, Lincoln's friend and the United States marshal for the District of Columbia, reported that Lincoln prepared a warrant to arrest Taney, but that went nowhere and Lamon's memory of the event has been doubted.[13] In any event, Taney's order was disregarded by everyone, including the courts. Rather than ask the marshals to enforce it, Taney simply sent a copy of it to Lincoln, knowing he would ignore it. For his part, Lincoln might have appealed the decision, but instead let it lie and had Merryman quietly released a few months later.[14]

Over the next few years, the Lincoln administration suppressed the civil liberties of northern "copperheads" who opposed the war. The secretary of war, Edwin Stanton, detained thirteen thousand civilians during its course, and had scores of newspapers shut down. The *Chicago Daily Times* editorialized that "it cannot be possible that a Christian nation can desire to see thousands and tens of thousands of their people and tens of thousands of a kindred people butchered, and all the expenses and horrors of a civil war incurred without some adequate motive."[15] Some would have found that persuasive, but Stanton seized the newspaper's presses, as he did those of the *New York Morning News*, the *Philadelphia Evening Journal* and many other papers.

Lincoln is properly remembered as a champion of democracy, but there was a good bit of Otto von Bismarck in him as well. Both men had unified their countries, at about the same time, through an assertion of naked force that dispensed with liberal scrupulosities. Crucially, both succeeded.

We forgive Lincoln's assumption of extreme powers because this might have been necessary to conduct a civil war. We forgive it because America's civil liberties and size of government snapped back in place after the war.[16] We forgive it because Lincoln was entirely without the streak of cruelty that marks a tyrant, because he preserved the world's then greatest democracy, and because he ran for reelection in 1864 even though he thought he would lose. We forgive it because fate made him a martyr to liberty. We forgive it, mostly, because Lincoln won the war and freed the slaves. But had it turned out differently, had Lee won the Battle of Gettysburg and marched on Washington, had hundreds of thousands of deaths failed to reunite the country, had slavery endured and had Lincoln lived on to the mediocrities of old age, we might remember him as the worst of our presidents. If you think otherwise, your hindsight bias is showing.

And now? Were a state to secede today, we would have two presidential models to choose from, Buchanan and Lincoln. Buchanan is remembered as a weak-minded failure, but is it so certain that we'd want to see a Lincoln in office, ready to use any means necessary to preserve the Union, ready to sacrifice the lives of many thousands of soldiers? It's not 1861 anymore. Back then, the southern secession ordinances proclaimed that the issue was slavery.[17] And as Lincoln said in his second inaugural address, everyone knew that slavery was somehow the cause of the war. Thus his decision to resist disunion was clothed with a moral authority that it otherwise would have lacked, and which would be wholly absent if a state chose to secede today.

Twenty-first-century America wouldn't want a president with Lincoln's Bismarckian approach to holding the country together. In a recent Gallup poll, only 44 percent expressed a willingness to fight for their country, and the number would likely be far lower if one group of Americans were asked to fight another, when the moral issues are so much less compelling than slavery. Rather than fight a civil war over a California secession, most people would likely prefer the exit option. Nearly sixty thousand Californians left the state for Texas each year on average between 2011 and 2015, and the numbers could swell with a Calexit. Progressive Texans might be inspired to move the other direction to an independent Republic of California. Unionists across the country would probably rather subsidize U-Haul rental fees than get into a war with fellow Americans. We're a mobile country, so asking people to move wouldn't look like a great imposition, and would be much easier to swallow than sending in a General Sherman.

We would also object to Lincoln's willingness to rule extra-constitutionally for the sake of preserving the Union. That made him a "commissary dictator," one who suspends the constitution in order to protect it, said the German legal philosopher Carl Schmitt.[18] Lincoln himself acknowledged how extraordinary were the powers he had asserted, in a message to Congress on July 4, 1861. Yes, he had suspended the writ of habeas corpus, even though he had sworn to take care that the laws be faithfully executed. But there were many laws he was bound to uphold, and he asked, "are all the laws, but one, to go unexecuted, and the government itself go to pieces, lest that one be violated? Even in such a case, would not the official oath be broken, if the government should be overthrown, when it was believed that disregarding the single law, would tend to preserve it?"

Lincoln thought that the secession crisis of 1861 was an exception to constitutional governance that justified departures from its laws. That made him America's sovereign, in the famous definition Schmitt gave to that word: "Sovereign is he who decides on the exception."[19] Sovereignty, so defined, is what Buchanan disclaimed, however, when he thought that the question of how to respond to the seceding states lay with Congress. And wouldn't we think him right, if the issue arose again on a Calexit? And wasn't Buchanan also right, in his last State of the Union message, in thinking that the Union should not be preserved by military might?

> The fact is that our Union rests upon public opinion, and can never be cemented by the blood of its citizens shed in civil war. If it can not live in the affections of the people, it must one day perish. Congress possesses many means of preserving it by conciliation, but the sword was not placed in their hand to preserve it by force.

The Con-Con

Before we see a state brought back by force into the Union, we would likely try to find a peaceful means of resolving the crisis. One possibility would be for the seceding state to abandon its quest for independence. Or we might bring about a peaceful separation through a constitutional convention, a Con-Con, under Article V of the Constitution.

Assuming that the Constitution bans a unilateral act of secession, a state might nevertheless be permitted to exit the Union through a constitutional amendment. There are two ways of doing so. The principal method, and the only way in which we've amended the Constitution until now, is through congressional action ratified by three-fourths (thirty-eight) of the states. The other method, adopted at the suggestion of George Mason at the Philadelphia Convention of 1787, involves a constitutional convention called by the legislatures of two-thirds (thirty-four) of the states. The federal government would never agree to give up its powers, said Mason, but the states might make it happen through such a convention. An amendment proposed by that means would become effective when ratified by thirty-eight states in a subsequent convention.[20]

Con-Cons represent one of the most fundamental ideas about American government: that here the people are sovereign. John Locke also believed that sovereignty vests in the people, but he thought this sovereignty could be asserted only when the government is dissolved.[21] That might be true in Britain, but in America the Constitution itself contemplates the possibility of revolutionary change through a constitutional convention that sidesteps Congress. James Wilson, a Pennsylvania delegate at the Philadelphia Convention, could therefore argue that the "revolution principle—that, the sovereign power residing in the people; they may change their constitution and their government whenever they please—is not a principle of discord, rancour or war: it is a principle of melioration, contentment, and peace."[22]

Theories about sovereignty might seem far removed from day-to-day politics, but under the radar the sneaky conservatives at Arizona's Goldwater Institute have been quietly laboring for a Con-Con. Far from the gaze of the *New Yorker*, they've been persuading state legislators to call for an Article V convention, and they're close to success. At least twenty-eight state legislatures have called for such a convention in order to consider a balanced budget amendment. More than six other states have called for a convention to consider other proposals. If we could lump them all together we'd have the thirty-four states required under Article V.[23]

As for what would happen then, the sky's the limit. We might have a "runaway convention" that takes up the question of secession, since nothing in Article V suggests any limits on what the convention may agree to.[24] In fact, the Framers' own Philadelphia Convention was a classic example of a runaway convention. They were sent to tinker with the Articles of Confederation, and instead they came up with a wholly new constitution. The Goldwater Institute itself recommends that state legislators give convention delegates "a meaningful level of deliberative independence to ensure that the amendments convention can serve its consensus-building and problem-solving purpose."[25]

In a crisis, therefore, state legislators might try to resolve the question of secession without bringing Congress into the picture. And that's what happened just before the Civil War began, when the Virginia legislature called upon other states to join them in a Peace Convention. This was greeted as the last chance to settle differences, and the delegates met at the Willard Hotel in Washington in February 1861. There were 131 of them, from twenty-one of the thirty-three states, and they included many of the country's most distinguished elder statesmen. Virginia sent a former president, John Tyler, who was chosen as the convention's president. From New York came David Dudley Field, law reformer, and Erastus Corning, president of New York Central Railroad. A future chief justice, Salmon P. Chase, represented Ohio. Reverdy Johnson, the former U.S. attorney general, led the Maryland delegation, and other states sent their chief justices, congressmen and former governors.

The Peace Convention is an object lesson in the difficulty of getting the genie of secession back into the bottle once it is released. Certainly, many Americans were willing to compromise in order to avoid war. William Seward, who would become Lincoln's secretary of state, was against slavery but said that "the question of slavery is not now to be taken into account. We must save the union."[26] He proposed a thirteenth constitutional amendment to guarantee the security of slavery in the states—not to abolish slavery, as the Thirteenth Amendment would do in 1865. For his part, Lincoln signaled in his first inaugural address that he would be content with such a measure.

None of this satisfied the southerners, however. The differences over the extension of slavery into the territories were too great to be overcome, and northern delegates wondered if the southerners were acting in good faith. President Buchanan stayed away from the Peace Convention, while Lincoln remained in Springfield until February 11 and then began a long, circuitous rail trip that brought him to Washington only when the convention was on the verge of failure. When it was over, Tyler returned to Virginia to argue for secession.

Why the Peace Convention failed might seem puzzling, since the southerners had everything they could reasonably have wanted—but for one thing. No one could force the northerners to like slavery or respect the slaveholders. At the convention, James Seddon of Virginia complained that they had been assailed, attacked, vilified and defamed by the northerners, and that this was intolerable. "We of Virginia must have in this Confederation the position of an equal," Seddon declared. "...Otherwise we are a dishonored people.... We hold our *property*, yes our *property in slaves*, as rightful and as honorable as any property to be found in the broad expanse between ocean and ocean."[27] But the respect he wanted, the North could not give him, and shortly thereafter he became the Confederate secretary of war.

Respect is something we all crave, just as much as Seddon did, but we have little respect for each other today. America is as divided as it was during the Peace Convention of 1861, and if history is a guide it's unlikely that a state would be pulled back from secession by a constitutional convention. More likely, the delegates would agree to let the seceding state depart in peace, overcoming any constitutional barriers to disunion. A California that asks to secede might even be met with a heartland that answers, "Don't let the door hit you on the way out." Or perhaps, "You're not leaving us. We're leaving you!" If the alternative is armed conflict, that has to be a less painful solution.

Exiting the Victor's Constitution

As a political matter, the question of secession was seemingly settled at Appomattox Court House in 1865. As a constitutional matter, the Supreme Court concurred, both by upholding Lincoln's military moves against the Confederacy during the Civil War,[28] and by expressly denying a right of secession afterward.[29] But the Framers had a different idea when they wrote our Constitution. They regarded what they were drafting as a compact among the states, with exit rights if states thought things weren't working out. This was forgotten at Appomattox, however. The flat rejection of secession rights can thus be seen as a victor's constitution, and were the Court to reexamine the constitutionality of secession today, it would likely take a more nuanced view of exit rights, one that leaves wiggle room for disunion. In particular, originalists on the Court who are faithful to the intentions of the Framers would be willing to recognize secession rights.

What Did the Framers Think?

The Framers clearly contemplated the possibility of secession. The Articles of Confederation, under which they were governed, created "a firm league of friendship" among the states, which retained their sovereignty to the extent that it had not been delegated to the United States. True, the Articles provided "that the Union shall be perpetual," but none of the delegates thought this would prevent a breakup. Whatever government might exist, said Alexander Hamilton, was "dissolving or already dissolved" by 1787.[30] During the Revolution, the thirteen colonies had joined forces to fight the British, but now there was no foreign enemy to unite them. No one thought they were much constrained by the Articles of Confederation, which states and leaders such as George Washington blithely ignored when it suited them.

At several points during the Constitutional Convention, the delegates expected that they would fail to agree, and that the country would break up into different sections. James Madison, whom scholars mistakenly call the father of the Constitution, seems to have proposed a walkout in the middle of the convention.[31] And then the Union might have split apart. Nathaniel Gorham from Massachusetts "conceived that a rupture of the Union wd. be an event unhappy for all, but surely the large States would be least unable to take care of themselves."[32] Madison anticipated that a dissolution of the Union would lead to the creation of "partial confederacies," and warned of the danger that some of them would immediately ally themselves with rival European powers.[33] Connecticut's Oliver Ellsworth and James Wilson, both future Supreme Court justices, thought a breakup of the country was possible if the delegates could not agree on how to amend the Articles of Confederation.[34] That was also how Hamilton saw things in *Federalist* 6. No one believed that the "perpetual" union under the Articles would prevent a breakup.

The delegates thought of the government under the Articles of Confederation, and then under the Constitution they were drafting, as a *compact* among thirteen states, and they believed that when one state thought its rights had been traduced by the federal government it could withdraw from the compact, even as one party can rescind a contract when the other party has breached it. That's what Madison argued, first in the Constitutional Convention,[35] then in *Federalist* 43 and then in the Virginia Ratifying Convention. It was an argument he would repeat in drafting the 1798 Virginia Resolutions. In its ratifying convention, Virginia reserved the right to secede when the powers granted to the federal government had been perverted, to the injury or oppression of the state.[36] That, said Madison, would safeguard Virginia should it object to the federal government.[37] So Virginia's ratification of the Constitution was expressly conditioned on a right of secession. How then could it be deemed unconditional?

The constitutional originalist must therefore conclude that states have a right to secede. That's what the New England Federalists must have thought when they objected to the War of 1812 and flirted with secession at the 1814 Hartford Convention.[38] Not everyone agreed before the Civil War, mind you. As we saw, Buchanan rejected the compact theory, and so did Lincoln in his first inaugural address. Before the Civil War, Joseph Story and Daniel Webster had also argued that the Union could not be unilaterally dissolved. But the question was very much an open one, and people like Robert E. Lee and Jefferson Davis did not think they were committing treason against the United States by adhering to their new country in the South.

The Trial of Jefferson Davis

I once brought Gordon Wood, eminent historian of eighteenth-century America, to the Robert E. Lee House in Alexandria. It was where Lee had lived as a boy, and Alexandria was where he had studied at the local free school and worshipped at Christ Church on nearby Washington Street. The house featured the scroll of a congressional resolution that retroactively granted Lee his citizenship. Lee had sought to have it restored before he died, as part of his mission to mend old wounds, but a government clerk had apparently deep-sixed the application. And so, in a bicentennial moment, Congress repaired the omission. The resolution described Lee in the most glowing terms, commending him for his courage, his integrity, his loyalty. "Loyalty!" exclaimed Gordon. "The man was a traitor!"

Well, yes, there was that unpleasantness over the Civil War. But was he a traitor?

In 1865 the victors weren't quite sure what to do with the defeated Confederates. Lee's surrender at Appomattox was the most civilized of affairs, and General Grant behaved with the magnanimity of the Black Prince after the Battle of Poitiers. The code of military chivalry demanded no less, and Grant subsequently ensured that Lee would not be tried for treason. But the politicians were another matter.

Lincoln would have been only too happy to see the Confederate cabinet escape to another country. Some in fact did so. Judah P. Benjamin, who had been a U.S. senator before the war, and served as the Confederate secretary of state, secretary of war and attorney general, made his way to England. There he read for the bar, and while doing so he wrote a legal treatise that is still in print.[39] As a leading barrister, he took constitutional cases from Canada to the Judicial Committee of the Privy Council, where he argued for the provinces against the federal government. In this he was so successful that it was said of him that he had proposed the doctrine of states' rights in two countries, failed in the first and succeeded in the second.

Jefferson Davis was not so lucky. He too had been a U.S. senator before the war, and also served as Franklin Pierce's secretary of war. After the war he fled south along with Benjamin, but was captured and placed in leg irons. He was indicted for treason and remained in a military prison for two years, until he was released on $100,000 bail. That would have been an impossibly large sum for Davis, but it was ponied up by twenty sympathizers, including Horace Greeley.

Davis was never tried on the charge. He demanded a trial by jury to prove that the South had the right to secede, but Andrew Johnson amnestied him, along with everyone else who had participated in the rebellion, before the case could be heard. The country had adopted the Reconstruction Amendments and wanted to put the war behind it. And then there was the fear that the prosecution would fail. What if Davis won and the Supreme Court held that there was a right of secession? In that case, the country might have to go through the whole thing again!

In prosecuting Davis, President Johnson faced the same kind of barriers that had stymied Buchanan in 1860. The treason, if that's what it was, had been committed in Virginia, and Davis would therefore be tried in that state. But no jury of ordinary Virginians could have been found to convict their former president.[40] When he was released from prison, a voice cried out "Hats Off, Virginians," and five thousand bareheaded men paid silent homage to Davis.[41]

There was also the ingenious argument that the trial would amount to double jeopardy, since Davis had already been barred from taking public office by the Fourteenth Amendment. You can't be tried twice for the same crime. But the bar against holding public office was nothing like a criminal penalty. Remarkably, it was Chief Justice Salmon Chase who came up with the specious argument of double jeopardy and who whispered it into the ear of Davis's lawyer. The Supreme Court reserved judgment, with Chase signaling that he agreed with the plea of double jeopardy.[42] The politically astute chief justice wanted the case to go away, as it soon did with President Johnson's amnesty proclamation. In 1868 everyone wanted a fresh start, and so there was no trial of Jefferson Davis.

The Supreme Court had reacted to Lincoln's conduct of the war in a highly politicized manner. While the war was ongoing, the Court did not object to the president's suspension of habeas corpus, but when the South was good and properly beaten and the matter was moot, it held that the suspension had been unconstitutional.[43] Similarly, when the trial of Jefferson Davis might have proved embarrassing, Chase managed to dodge the issue. In the very next year, however, the Court held in *Texas v. White* that secession was unconstitutional.[44]

That case concerned the status of Texas bonds issued to finance the Confederate war effort. These, said the Court, were void, as was the Texas act of secession itself. The Articles of Confederation, by which the states were united in 1781, affirmed that the union was perpetual. When the Articles were replaced by the Constitution, said the Court, this was only "to form a more perfect union," which meant that the quality of perpetuity survived and that the new union must be no less permanent. When Texas joined the United States, it was as a perpetual member of an indissoluble union. The bonds issued by Texas after seceding were therefore void, and that was final.

That wasn't how the Framers had seen things, and it's not what Jefferson Davis and Robert E. Lee thought in 1861. After the Civil War, a politicized Supreme Court discovered a principle of perpetual union. Insofar as this represents a victor's constitution, it would be a less than reliable authority if Secession 2.0 were to come before the Court.

A Middle Way

Suppose that the question is not what is to be done with a subjugated state such as the Texas of 1869, but prospectively, before a war has begun, when a state such as California seeks to secede and when a civil war threatens. In that case, would we expect the Supreme Court to ignore the very different political circumstances in which the question arises? Would we want it to arm a president with all the authority that Lincoln commanded during the Civil War? Or might we expect a Court, composed in part of originalists and never entirely indifferent to politics, to recall how the Framers thought that secession might be permitted? Might they think that there are values more fundamental than preserving the Union, such as adherence to democratic rule, when a state has voted for secession?

The decision would be a difficult one, and the Court would likely wish to reflect on how the Canadian Supreme Court ruled on secession rights in its *Reference re Secession of Quebec.*[45] In Canada, unlike the United States, the government can submit a question for resolution by the Supreme Court in the absence of underlying litigation. And the question of secession was no mere hypothetical one, after the separatist Parti Québécois was elected in that province in 1976.

In 1980, the Quebec government had sought the authority to negotiate what it called sovereignty-association in an opaque 106-word referendum question. The referendum asked Quebeckers to permit the government to negotiate a new agreement with Canada, with sovereignty for the province but with an undefined financial association with the rest of Canada, and with a further secession referendum if the negotiations failed. The wording enraged Quebec federalists, especially in the English-speaking minority, who said that the question's lack of clarity obscured the issue,[46] that it falsely suggested that Quebeckers could have their cake and eat it too, that the Quebec government would negotiate in bad faith, blame the rest of Canada and then conduct a snap referendum on secession.

The referendum failed, however, as (very narrowly) did another referendum in 1995. That second referendum was forty-three words long and asked for a mandate for Quebec sovereignty, again in murky language that might not have seemed threatening. Had the referendum passed, however, the French government was reportedly ready to recognize Quebec as an independent country the next day. That might have sufficed to establish the province's independence, even as French recognition of an independent America was so crucial in our successful revolution.

The manner in which the Parti Québécois had sought the authority to declare the province independent, through confusing referendum questions, prompted the Supreme Court reference. Under Canadian constitutional law, referenda themselves lack legal force, but Canadian governments have nevertheless employed them to lend legitimacy to parliamentary legislation, and did so over military conscription in the Second World War. The federal government therefore asked the Supreme Court to rule on the circumstances in which a province could secede. How clear must a referendum question be? Did the Quebec National Assembly have the power to secede, with or without a referendum? Was there a right to unilateral secession under principles of self-determination in international law?

The Court began by stating that the right of secession under constitutional law raised the broadest of questions.

> The Constitution is more than a written text. It embraces the entire global system of rules and principles which govern the exercise of constitutional authority. A superficial reading of selected provisions of the written constitutional enactment, without more, may be misleading. It is necessary to make a more profound investigation of the underlying principles animating the whole of the Constitution, including the principles of federalism, democracy, constitutionalism and the rule of law, and respect for minorities. Those principles must inform our overall appreciation of the constitutional rights and obligations that would come into play in the event that a clear majority of Quebecers votes on a clear question in favour of secession.

There was not, in short, an easy *yes* or *no* answer to Quebec's assertion of secession rights. A democratic vote for secession demanded respect, because democracy was a ground norm of the Canadian constitution. A successful democratic referendum would not give Quebec a unilateral right of secession, however. In a federal state, whose provinces have close ties of interdependence, the votes of people in other provinces count too.

Nor could the province invoke a right of self-determination under international law. Such a right might exist when its government represents the whole of its people, on a basis of equality and without discrimination, and when it is oppressed by a colonial power. That's what the United Nations favors, and that's how the Soviet Union broke up. But this didn't help Quebec, for its people were not united and it wasn't colonized. There were linguistic, religious and cultural differences among Quebeckers, and it could not be said that anyone was oppressed by the federal government.

The Canadian Court would also have required a satisfactory division of federal assets in the province and an assumption by the seceding province of its portion of the national debt.[47] Since Canada's name is on the debt obligations it issued, the country would be fully liable for payment if a province seceded. But this would be unjust to the country from which it exited, and would amount to a bankruptcy petition. It would also give the exiting state a wasteful incentive to secede, like the traveler who skips town without paying his hotel bill. That was something of which the Americans were well aware in 1776, and in case they had forgotten, Tom Paine reminded them of it in *Common Sense*. The Seven Years' War had doubled Britain's public debt to £140 million, on which it paid £4 million a year in interest. But an independent America would be debt-free, said Paine, and could more cheaply build its own navy than subsidize the Royal Navy. In the circumstances, the British connection was a financial burden for Americans and independence would be profitable.[48]

That was not the end of the matter, however, since the Court held that a successful referendum question would ground the right of Quebec to initiate constitutional change, and the correlative duty of the other provinces and the federal government "to engage in discussions to address any legitimate initiative to change the constitutional order." A clear majority vote on a clear question in favor of secession "would confer democratic legitimacy on the secession initiative which all of the other participants in Confederation would have to recognize." The parties would then be obliged to negotiate the terms of disunion, taking into account the interests of all parties, the rights of all Canadians both within and outside Quebec and particularly the rights of minorities. In American terms, that would mean a constitutional convention.

The Canadian Court therefore rejected both an abstract right of secession, as the Confederacy had asserted, and an absolute ban on secession, as ruled in *Texas v. White*. Suppose that the U.S. Supreme Court were today faced with the question of secession on a Calexit. Would it embrace the middle way of the Canadian Supreme Court?

First, it is inconceivable that a court would adopt the Confederacy's compact theory and a unilateral right of secession. Even if the Framers might have subscribed to it, no court would permit an exit where the seceding state would mistreat minority groups. It's all very well to say that such an outcome wouldn't happen now, that black Americans would have nothing to fear in today's South, but this argument recognizes the same conditions on secession rights that the Canadian Supreme Court adopted. If southern states had the abstract right to secede without conditions, they could do so today even if they proposed to deal with minorities as they had in 1861.

In the other corner is the absolute bar on secession seen in *Texas v. White*, and today that also seems extreme. Imagine a clear vote for secession in a state, passed by an overwhelming majority. To say that this is a nullity which the federal government could ignore is to say that the president could send in the army to suppress it, dissolve the state assembly, imprison secessionists and make war on the state. Is our devotion to the Union so absolute that it must be preserved in blood? Would we want to hand a loaded pistol to a Lincolnian president, permitting him to go to war without regard to what Congress and the courts might think? In his 1860 message to Congress, James Buchanan said that this would be "a naked act of usurpation," and that he was required to submit the question of secession to Congress. If the matter were to arise again, would you say that Buchanan was wrong and Lincoln was right?

The moral case against secession is far weaker today than it was in 1861, and the Canadian middle way would therefore be appealing as a reasonable compromise. The U.S. Supreme Court would be asked to decide which value is more fundamental: the preservation of the Union with an absolute barrier to secession, or the commitment to democratic norms and the protection of citizens from invasion and harm.

A state's act of secession, after an overwhelming *yes* vote on a clearly worded referendum, must begin a process of negotiations between it and the federal government, and it's difficult to imagine an American president shutting his ears to the need for discussions and compromises. As for what would emerge from this, who can say? Perhaps a compromise that preserves the Union, perhaps not. The Parti Québécois's notion of sovereignty-association was not a bad one, had it been feasible. We might concede the seceding state's independence in general, while maintaining some form of association between it and the rest of America. That might include, for example, the free movement of goods, services and people. But all this would depend on the negotiations and would lie in the realm of politics. It would be contingent upon events difficult to foresee—such as whether the seceding state would be recognized as independent by the French government.

In any case, the barriers to secession are far lower than most would imagine, and the temptation to split apart is far greater than at any time since 1860. So it's time to think seriously about Secession 2.0 as a possibility.

PART II

~

A CURE FOR BIGNESS?

It is the vice of a vulgar mind to be thrilled by bigness.
— E. M. Forster, *Howards End*

4

BIGNESS AND BADNESS

At different times in our past we've come close to a breakup. At the 1787 Philadelphia Convention, many of the Framers thought the country would split apart if they couldn't compromise on a constitution. In 1860–61 the southern states began to secede, and before Fort Sumter the better thinking was that they would be allowed to go. Now we're hearing rumbles for secession again.

We could put today's talk of secession down to the partisan animosities that stem from the 2016 election, but perhaps there's a simpler reason. Perhaps we're just too damn big. After China and India, we're the third largest country by population. There are no secessionist movements in China, but that's only because the country is governed by a Communist regime that brutally suppressed the Tibetan independence movement and has interned hundreds of thousands of Uyghurs in the western Xinjiang region. India is democratic, but on its creation in 1947 it was riven by the secession of Pakistan and a civil war, and since then it has used its military to quell separatist discontent in Assam and the Punjab.

Go down the list of the ten most populous countries and you'll find separatist movements in Indonesia, Pakistan, Nigeria, Bangladesh and Russia. Go down a bit further and you'll find active separatist movements in Iraq, the Philippines and Turkey. Cyprus has remained divided on an ethnic and religious basis since 1974, and even Australia might have split apart in 1933 but for the refusal of the British government to take seriously a successful secession referendum in Western Australia. Ireland's quest for independence from Britain was a secession movement, and today there is a strong drive for Scottish secession.

With a large population, there's a greater likelihood that a country will have the kind of diversity that might spark a secession movement, and the same might be said of countries that are large in area. By land mass, America is the fourth largest country in the world. Both Russia and Canada are larger, and there are secession movements in both. China is also larger, and a good example of the repression a country might require to still the demand for a breakaway.

America is large in population and in geographical size. What reason have we to expect that we alone, of all the world's large countries, will remain unified and resist separatist movements? Perhaps some countries are simply too big, and maybe the United States is one of them.

The Friends of David Hume

What the right size for a state might be was debated by three of the eighteenth century's greatest thinkers. David Hume argued for bigness, while Montesquieu (Charles-Louis de Secondat) and Jean-Jacques Rousseau made the case for smallness. In the eighteenth century's Republic of Letters, all three knew each other. With Montesquieu, Hume carried on a respectful correspondence. With Rousseau, Hume had a deep friendship that turned into the nastiest of personal squabbles.

David Hume was a man of his time, and his time was the Enlightenment. He was quite without political or religious enthusiasms, and his *History of England* annoyed British Whigs with his sympathy for the Stuart monarchs. With his skepticism about traditional religious belief and contempt for what he called mere superstition, he also shocked his pious countrymen. James Boswell visited him on his deathbed, to see whether the notorious infidel would express a desire for an afterlife. Not at all, answered Hume. The thought of annihilation on death no more disturbed him than the idea that he had not existed before being born. Boswell later recalled the conversation with the good-humored philosopher. "'Well,' said I, 'Mr. Hume, I hope to triumph over you when I meet you in a future state; and remember you are not to pretend that you was joking with all this infidelity.' 'No, no,' said he. 'But I shall have been so long there before you come that it will be nothing new.'"[1]

Boswell thought him Britain's greatest writer, and he was certainly the country's greatest philosopher. In 1739, at age twenty-seven, Hume published *The Treatise of Human Nature*, the book that Immanuel Kant said had awakened him from his dogmatic slumber and that prompted him to write the *Critique of Pure Reason* to answer Hume. But Kant published his book more than forty years after Hume's treatise, which in its own day, said Hume, "fell *dead-born from the press.*"[2]

That seemed to be a false start, so Hume turned next to political philosophy, with a remarkable series of essays that appeared in 1741–42 and anticipated many of the issues that the Framers discussed. In one essay, published before Montesquieu's *Spirit of the Laws*, he defended the separation of powers of the "balanced" British constitution, of king, lords and commons.[3] In another essay, he demolished the idea that our duty of allegiance to a state might be grounded in a social contract, the hypothetical bargain in which we agreed to emerge from a pregovernmental state of nature into civil society, according to Hobbes and Locke. There never was such a bargain, said Hume, and even if there had been, it could not ground obedience to the state in the present since we would never have had any choice but to consent to it.[4] Then, in a third essay, Hume proposed a system of refinement or filtration of elected officials that strongly influenced the Framers in general and Madison in particular. If voters elected a lower set of representatives who from among themselves then elected a higher senate and so on up the ladder, only the wisest and most virtuous leaders would rise to the top. Lesser mortals would be filtered away.

These ideas on government were so original and rich that it's easy to understand why Don Livingston became a Hume scholar, although as a secessionist Livingston disagrees with one of Hume's ideas, that people are better off in bigger states. Large republics are protected from "tumult and faction," said Hume, since their very size makes it harder for factions or interest groups to coalesce and oppose the public good. "The parts are so distant and remote, that it is very difficult, either by intrigue, prejudice, or passion, to hurry them into any measures against the public interest."[5] So America might have a local Virginia tobacco lobby or a Massachusetts cod lobby, but those local lobbies could never overcome geography and unite across the entire country, according to Hume's theory.

What Hume was describing is what today's economists call the *collective action* problem. Sometimes you need a group of people to get things done, and the more members in the group, the harder it is to come to agreement. The greater the number of people, the more likely you'll find someone who wants to hold out. It's always tempting to let someone else do it, and when the group is large it's easier to get away with this.[6] When I was in law practice, our firm had a financially stressed client that sought a composition with its international creditors, in which each was asked to accept something less than 100 cents on the dollar. Most of them went along with it, but one foreign creditor insisted on payment in full. *Pay the rest of them 60 cents*, it said. *We want 100 cents on the dollar*. When one creditor said this, the others then wanted full payment as well, and so the greediness of a single holdout made it impossible to come to a deal.

The collective action problem gets in the way of good projects getting done, and that's unfortunate. What Hume had in mind, however, was the way in which the collective action problem might serve a useful purpose, if we wouldn't want the group to be formed. One example of this is a cartel of producers that would harm consumers by monopolizing the market and fixing prices. Another is an interest group that would promote its own private advantage through legislation that is harmful to the public good. We'd want such groups to fail, and Hume said that in a larger state they would be less likely to get organized in the first place. A large country such as Britain might thus be well governed, he thought. So bigger might be better—at least up to a point.[7]

Montesquieu thought the opposite, that small states would be better governed.[8] His *Spirit of the Laws* was published in 1748, and became one of the best-known eighteenth-century works on political philosophy. Like Hume, the French author feared the influence of factions or interest groups, but he thought there would be fewer of them in small states. People would know each other better and wouldn't feel the need to organize into groups to promote their particular interests.

"The public good is better sensed, better understood, closer to each citizen" in small states, according to Montesquieu.[9]

That was one argument for smallness, but Montesquieu had a second one, which concerns the corrupting influence of wealth and the arrogance and indifference of the super-rich. There would be greater personal fortunes in large republics, and the super-wealthy wouldn't have the sense that we're all in this together, so they would care less about their country. As Montesquieu put it, "A man will first feel that he can be happy, great, and glorious without his country; and shortly that he can be happy over the ruins of his country."

That was Montesquieu's explanation for the fall of Rome, in his *Grandeur of the Romans and Their Decadence* (1734). Rome's greatness came from its smallness, he said, and the bigness of the Roman Empire proved fatal. When Rome was a small city-state, its citizens all had the same magistrates, the same gods, the same love of liberty. Crucially, the land was equally divided among its citizens. There were no great disparities of wealth, and everyone had a similar and weighty interest in defending his city. That made Rome's armies powerful. But when the city expanded across Italy, the sense of common identity faded. Each Italian town had its own interests, its own gods, its own leading families, and Roman citizenship became little more than a legal fiction.[10] Great estates arose and the country was divided between luxury-loving landowners on the one hand and a race of slaves and artisans on the other. Both classes were cowardly and corrupt, and neither could provide the country with the soldiers it needed. The Roman Empire was forced to rely on armies of mercenaries from beyond Italy who had no allegiance to anyone but their commanders, who would become the new emperors.[11]

As a city-state, Rome had fostered a virtuous citizenry, which had made it powerful, leading to conquest and expansion into a great empire. But this in turn corrupted Roman virtue and left the empire at the mercy of invading barbarians. Rome was a victim of its own success. The great mistake was bigness.

Jean-Jacques Rousseau came to a similar conclusion about the dangers of bigness in his *Considerations on the Government of Poland* (1782): "Greatness of Nations. Size of States! The first and principal source of the miseries of mankind." In small states, the citizens know and keep watch over each other, and the rulers can observe how the laws are carried out. Large states, by contrast, are "crushed by their own mass," and groan under either anarchy or oppression.[12]

Hume came from a poor but professional family, and attended the University of Edinburgh. Montesquieu was a member of the French nobility and the president of the Bordeaux parliament. Rousseau came from a humbler milieu. His father was a watchmaker, and from him Rousseau inherited the artisan's resentment of aristocratic polish and culture. Hume never met Montesquieu, but he did meet Rousseau, befriended him and became his most generous patron.

Hume brought Rousseau to England when he was expelled by the Swiss, and arranged for a generous pension from George III. Rousseau always craved attention, and he often got it. When Hume brought him to the theater to see the celebrated actor David Garrick in Voltaire's *Zaire*, Rousseau leaned so far outside the box that everyone thought he must fall, and watched him rather than Garrick. In the audience, even George III peered at him through opera glasses.[13]

Eventually Rousseau said he wanted quiet, and Hume found a country gentleman to take him in. But very quickly the paranoid and ungrateful Rousseau accused Hume of spreading lies about him, of bringing him to England only to betray him.[14] It was one of the greatest philosophical dust-ups of all time. It couldn't have helped that Hume's friend James Boswell had seduced Rousseau's mistress—who proceeded to give the bumptious Scot a master class in the art of love.[15]

Hume and Rousseau disagreed about the optimal size of a European state. But Hume wondered what might happen if the opportunity arose to start afresh, "either by a dissolution of some old government, or by the combination of men to form a new one, in some distant part of the world?" That hypothetical question became a real one when America subsequently dissolved its ties to a former government and the Framers in Philadelphia struggled to form a new one.

Roger Sherman's Constitution

For the Framers, the question about the optimal size of a state was one about the proper division of power between the federal and the state governments. Big is beautiful meant that power should be concentrated in a centralizing federal government. Small is beautiful meant a devolution of power to the states. In the debate, each side had its champion. James Madison argued for bigness and a powerful federal government, while Roger Sherman made the case for smallness and states' rights. In the end, it was smallness and the devolution of power to the thirteen states that won the day—not Madison's constitution, but Sherman's.

Madison had read Hume in college, and agreed with him that states should be large in size.[16] For the United States, that meant drawing power away from the states to the new federal government, and that's what Madison proposed in his Virginia Plan, which his state presented as the basis for a constitution at the Philadelphia Convention. He had outlined his thoughts on government in "Vices of the Political System of the United States," an essay written a month before the convention began.[17] The Articles of Confederation were too decentralized, he argued. The ultimate authority was left with the states, and the decisions of Congress were little more than recommendations. To remedy this, the new constitution must vest enormous power in the national government.

Hume had thought it would be harder for dangerous factions or interest groups to coalesce in a large country. Madison agreed, and he argued that in a large country the diverse interests would counterbalance each other. In an "extended republic," he wrote, "the Society becomes broken into a greater variety of interests, of pursuits, of passions, which check each other, whilst those who may feel a common sentiment have less opportunity of communication and concert." Big is beautiful, in short.

At the convention, Madison expanded upon the argument for bigness by describing how a majority of voters in a small state would oppress a minority. Centralizing power in the federal government would give us a large state with more diversity, where unjust majorities would be less likely to form. Connecticut might be majoritarian Congregationalist, but there would be no majority religious denomination in the United States as a whole. A strong federal government would therefore be the solution to the problem of faction, Madison argued:

> The only remedy is to enlarge the sphere, & thereby divide the
> community into so great a number of interests & parties, that in

the 1ˢᵗ place a majority will not be likely at the same moment to have a common interest separate from that of the whole or of the minority; and in the 2ᵈ place, that in case they shᵈ have such an interest, they may not be so apt to unite in the pursuit of it.[18]

The delegates at the convention weren't buying it, however. The ones from the small states, chiefly Roger Sherman of Connecticut, took Madison's ideas and turned them inside out. Sherman wasn't a political philosopher, and contented himself with saying that "the people are more happy in small than large states."[19] But he was a better politician than Madison, and he assembled a coalition of small-state delegates that opposed the nationalists. Madison wanted to give the federal government the right to veto state laws; he wouldn't get his way. He wanted a Senate dominated by the large states; he wouldn't get it. He wanted Congress to pick the president; he wouldn't get that either. Instead, the delegates voted for Roger Sherman's constitution, one in which small states would have a much stronger voice in the Senate and in the election of presidents. When Sherman and his small-state allies at the convention were finished, America would have a federal government in which power was tilted much more toward the states than Madison had wanted.

If conservatives have anyone to thank for the Constitution, it's Roger Sherman. Not only did he preserve federalism, by assembling a block of delegates to oppose Madison's federal veto power, but he gave us a Senate and an Electoral College in which small states are represented disproportionately. If Madison had gotten his way, seats in the Senate and votes in the Electoral College would be allocated by population. Al Gore would then have won the presidency in 2000, and Hillary Clinton in 2016.

When the convention was over, Madison knew he had lost. He wrote despairingly to Jefferson that "the plan...will neither effectually *answer* its *national object*, nor prevent the local *mischiefs* which everywhere *excite disgust* agst. the *State Governments*."[20] The country would be a federal state, or a "compound republic" as Madison called it in *Federalist* 51. Still, it wasn't all bad, which is why Madison and Hamilton wrote that selling document, *The Federalist Papers*.

America wouldn't be wholly one thing or another. It wouldn't have a unitary government where the states were nothing, and it wouldn't have the extremely weak central government provided by the Articles of Confederation. A federal state is also what Rousseau had suggested in his *Considerations on the Government of Poland.*[21] If a country couldn't be broken up into smaller countries, as he would have preferred, then perhaps sub-states could be created in a federal scheme of government.

With us, the choice isn't bigness versus smallness, but something in between. That was the promise of federalism. But the division of power between the large national government and the states has changed over time. In the beginning, the federal government was exceedingly small by today's standards. Then the balance of power shifted inexorably from the states to the federal government, which raises the question of who was right. Was it Hume and Madison for large republics and a strong federal government, or Montesquieu, Rousseau and Sherman for smaller governments and states' rights in a federal system?

Gouverneur Morris's Constitution

Quite apart from the division of powers between the federal government and the states, there's the question whether, for a large country like America, we have the right kind of federal government in Washington. What the Framers gave us is a presidential regime with a separation of powers between the executive, Senate and House of Representatives. This assumes that the different branches can get together to agree on needed legislative changes. But when Americans are as divided as they are today, the result is congressional gridlock and a dangerous shift of power to an imperial presidency, since it often takes executive diktats to get things done. We'd see less of that if we split apart, and that's an argument for secession.

It's to Gouverneur Morris, not James Madison, that we owe our separation of powers.[22] Until Morris stepped in, Madison and everyone else had wanted a president appointed by Congress. Like Hume, they thought that this would filter out the less-qualified people. Then Sherman and his small-state allies gave us a Senate where every state would have the same number of senators, who would be appointed by state governments. This meant that a congressionally appointed president would essentially be chosen by the states, and that wasn't acceptable to Morris. As a nationalist, he wanted to draw power away from the states to the federal government, and so he proposed the complicated machinery for choosing the president that we have in Article II of the Constitution. Today this means that presidents are elected by the people.

This is how we got an executive that's independent of the legislature, and why we need the separate concurrence of the president, the Senate and the House to get legislation passed. In the middle of the nineteenth century, Lord Macaulay complained that the American constitution, unlike that of Britain, was all sail and no anchor, too democratic and too quick to respond to demands for change.[23] But today the reality is just the opposite. In Britain, laws are easy to pass and easy to repeal in an all-powerful House of Commons. All you need is a majority government and some tough-minded party whips. It's in America that adopting new laws and repealing old ones is difficult. The constitutional separation of powers is all anchor.

It wasn't always so, because Republicans and Democrats weren't always so divided by ideological differences and partisan animosities as they are today. From 1946 to 1990, as many bills were passed in periods of divided government as when one party controlled both houses of Congress and the presidency.[24] But that's changed now. Between 2011 and 2017, when the Democrats held the White House and Republicans controlled Congress, it was understood that no major legislation could be passed. Gridlock was the order of the day, and it encouraged President Obama to ignore Congress and rule by decree. The separation of powers was meant to check an overpowerful president, but instead it has had the opposite effect, insulating him from accountability.[25]

As a consequence, we are now facing another constitutional crisis, as we did in the 1850s, when Congress was unable to compromise on slavery or avert the impending civil war. Today again, changes that must be made seemingly can't be made because of our divisions and failure to compromise. The Constitution was designed for another country, one in which people agreed on fundamental principles, and that's not today's America. We are divided on things that used to unite us, and we don't like politicians who compromise on issues we care about. We're also not so sure that we have the right kind of constitution.[26] Perhaps we've come to recognize that our Constitution requires a unity we no longer have, and that this makes secession more attractive.

5

BIGNESS AND HAPPINESS

The eighteenth-century debate about the optimal size of a state was full of clever theories, but it lacked the kind of empirical evidence that might back them up. Like most problems of political philosophy, the dispute was a factual one where the data was lacking. We could debate such questions till we're blue in the face: What's better, monarchies or republics? What's the best form of government, presidential or parliamentary?

When we can actually measure the parameters that enter into philosophical theories, the story changes. Today we have sophisticated ways to gather and analyze data on things like public corruption, and even happiness. And once the facts are in, smart people stop arguing. If we're asking what is the right size for a state, we have data pointing to an answer.

Take Roger Sherman's conjecture that people are happier in small states. Well, are they? To answer the question, we'd need to be able to compare different countries according to the happiness levels of the people who live there. Happily, the World Happiness Report tries to provide the data.

When you get down to it, is there a better way to rate countries than by the happiness of their people? Perhaps we have loftier goals for ourselves and for our families. We might aspire to something nobler than slothful contentment, something more virtuous. We also need to recognize how varied human pleasures are, and how they can be ranked on a qualitative scale. "It is better to be a human being dissatisfied than a pig satisfied," wrote John Stuart Mill. "Better to be Socrates dissatisfied than a fool satisfied."[1] That's how we would choose for ourselves, but we might not want the state to decide on our happiness for us, or to try to legislate us into Heaven. When that's been tried, it never works out very well.

If we had to write a program for our rulers, perhaps the best we could do is: "Create the conditions where people are happy." Or since we don't want the state to tell us when we're happy, "Create the conditions where people report that they're happy." There are obviously things a government can do that will make people more or less happy, and most of them are beyond the scope of this book. But if smaller countries are happier ones, then some large governments should permit their country to split apart.

Measuring Happiness

When countries do break into parts, as happened to the Soviet Union, the message is that people weren't very happy with things. Population flow also tells us a lot. When multitudes try to leave a country, such as Venezuela, that's a bad sign. When multitudes want to come into a country, such as the United States or Canada, that's a good sign. Building a wall to prevent people from leaving is a sign of failure. Building a wall to control the flow of people entering is a sign of success.

These are objective proxies for happiness, and there are other ones too, such as health and longevity. We would expect that people who are healthy and live longer are happier than those who are sick and die early, so we might look at longevity tables as one way of measuring happiness in a country. If longevity correlates with happiness, then China is a happier country than the United States, as are thirty other countries.[2]

In recent years, however, social scientists have measured happiness levels by asking people to report on their sense of well-being. Since 2012, the United Nations has published an annual World Happiness Report, in which people in member states are asked, "Overall, how satisfied are you with your life these days?" Respondents rate their own level of happiness on a scale of 0 to 10. These reports measure *subjective well-being* (SWB). According to the 2018 World Happiness Report, which included 154 countries, the United States is a much happier country than China.[3]

So we have an objective proxy measure, longevity, and a subjective one, and they give us different results. In general, economists regard subjective survey reports as distinctly second best. They give more weight to what is revealed in action than to what is reported—what people do rather than what they say. You might tell me that you like chocolate, but let's see how much of it you buy. Objective over subjective.

Favoring objective data over subjective reports makes sense, even when we are looking at something as subjective as personal preferences or feelings. There are various ways that broad comparisons of self-reported feelings can be misleading. A person might be embarrassed to report that he is unhappy, for example, and what he reports about his happiness today might not be what he remembers at a later date. Across different languages and cultures, people may not have the same understanding of a question about happiness, and their responses will differ accordingly.[4] There might be cultural differences regarding the value of happiness: is it shameful to be unhappy, or sinful to be happier than the less fortunate? A numerical scale doesn't solve that problem. The Irishman who puts himself down as seven out of ten on the scale might mean to say he's really pretty happy, that seven is as good as it gets. An Italian might assume that most people are at nine or ten, so if he answers seven it means he's rather gloomy. When one aggregates the responses and assigns a happiness level to an entire country, the uncertainties are magnified.

But while self-reported happiness levels are necessarily subjective and prone to ambiguity, people aren't likely to be self-deceived about their own happiness in the way they might be on other questions about themselves. In addition, a person's answers tend not to change much from one survey to the next, and people who describe themselves as happy tend to be so described by their friends. They are also more likely to make new friends and be helpful to others. People who report that they are very happy will smile more, while people who say they are unhappy exhibit more physiological signs of stress.[5] Finally, when we look at SWB reports for different countries, we see a correlation between reported happiness levels and conditions that we would expect to bear on happiness. People in war-torn countries are miserable, and the happiest people live in countries with well-developed economies. As far as empirical evidence of happiness goes, it doesn't get much better than SWB surveys.

So Who Is Happier?

Are people happier in big or small countries? When we look at the evidence from SWB surveys, we find that Sherman was right, along with Montesquieu and Rousseau, while Hume and Madison were wrong. People in small countries are happier. Bigness is badness.

Bigness can be measured either in geographic area or in population. The first mattered greatly in the Framers' time. When George Washington returned home at the end of the Constitutional Convention, it took him five days to get there.[6] Now the driving time between Philadelphia's Independence Hall and Mount Vernon is about three hours. In 1787, news traveled no more quickly than people. *The Federalist Papers* didn't much influence the ratification debates, as they were little read outside of New York.[7] All of this is utterly changed. Barriers to travel have shrunk, and barriers to communication have disappeared. Modern technology has annihilated distance.

If geography matters less today, population matters a lot. Let's consider how it applies to Madison's theory about factions diverting resources away from the public good. Today, interest groups can organize across a large geographic area much more easily than they could in the past. But a large population can present obstacles to building coalitions, since we're likely to see more ethnic, linguistic and political diversity with greater numbers of people. So we'll want to see whether the size of a country's population correlates with happiness levels.

Let's look at the evidence: As Table 5.1 shows, the happiest countries on the SWB scale are those with smaller populations. The United States comes in at number 18, and every country above us has fewer people—often much fewer. The happiest countries are disproportionately the small European ones, the Nordic countries, Switzerland, the Netherlands and so on.

TABLE 5.1 SUBJECTIVE WELL-BEING RANKINGS: HAPPIEST COUNTRIES

Ranking	Country	Population (000s)	SWB Happiness
1	Finland	5,495	7.63
2	Norway	5,233	7.59
3	Denmark	5,749	7.56
4	Iceland	334	7.50
5	Switzerland	8,372	7.49
6	Netherlands	17,201	7.44
7	Canada	36,918	7.33
8	New Zealand	4,693	7.32
9	Sweden	9,903	7.31
10	Australia	8,747	7.27
11	Israel	8,547	7.19
12	Austria	8,747	7.14
13	Costa Rica	4,857	7.07
14	Ireland	4,773	6.98
15	Germany	82,274	6.97
16	Belgium	11,491	6.93
17	Luxembourg	583	6.91
18	United States	326,510	6.89

Finland is at the top of the list, so why are the Finns so darned happy? It can't be the weather. Helsinki is "north of 60," the latitude where Canada's Northwest Territories begin, and way north of Juneau, Alaska. In the dead of winter Helsinki gets fewer than six hours of sunlight a day. And that's in Finland's far south. To the east, Finland is nestled against Russia, not the best of neighborhoods. Finland fought the Soviet Union in the Winter War of 1939–40, and until the fall of communism it deferred to the Soviets in foreign affairs.

Finland has its advantages, however. It's a parliamentary republic, relatively free from burdensome regulations, and one of the richest and least corrupt countries in the world. It also has the kind of social cohesion and unity that only small countries can have. Nearly 95 percent of Finns are native Finnish speakers, a language spoken nowhere else.

The country is just different. Its people enjoy cross-country skiing, Nordic walking and the national sport of pesäpallo (something like baseball). Finnish cuisine is heavy on buttermilk, lingonberries and turnips. If Finns belong to a church, it's almost certainly going to be

Lutheran. Because of the sense of unity, the country's cradle-to-grave social welfare system is popular with Finns.

What the Finns have going for them is a small population. If the country were twenty times bigger, it would be more diverse and less unified. Its leaders would be more remote from the people, and their policies more tainted by interest-group corruption. The country would be less happy. Madison's argument for bigness is therefore clearly flawed.

Now let's look at the most populous countries in Table 5.2. Apart from the United States, they're not especially happy, and the largest countries, China and India, are pretty morose. The United States is the great outlier. Population isn't everything, so we need to account for other variables too.

Plugging In More Factors

Many of the least happy countries are not very populous. According to the World Happiness Report, Burundi in sub-Saharan Africa (11.7 million people) is the unhappiest country in the world, even below war-torn Syria. In 2017, the UN Human Rights Commission documented "arbitrary arrests and detentions, acts of torture and cruel, inhuman or degrading treatment, extrajudicial executions, enforced disappearances, rape and other forms of sexual violence" in the country. No wonder that Burundians are so unhappy.

If we're going to make sense of the happiness data, then, we'll need to take account of much more than population size. Geographic size counts too, which we'll pick up by looking at population density (number of people divided by square mile). We'll also want to take regional differences into account. Many of the least happy countries are in sub-Saharan Africa, so we'll separate that region out. Similarly, Latin American countries have tended to be politically unstable and often have ruinous economic policies, so we'll break out that region too. The happiest countries are the most economically advanced—the countries of the Organization for Economic Cooperation and Development (OECD) and the BRICS countries (Brazil, Russia, India, China and South Africa)—so we'll want to consider them separately.

Ethnolinguistic differences can be a source of tension and even conflict in a country, and so we'll make this a variable. A high level of

TABLE 5.2 SUBJECTIVE WELL-BEING RANKINGS (OVER 200 MILLION PEOPLE)

Ranking	Country	Population (000s)	SWB Happiness
86	China	1,413	5.25
133	India	1,352	4.19
18	United States	327	6.89
96	Indonesia	266	5.09
28	Brazil	211	6.42
75	Pakistan	200	5.47
World Average			5.37
Sub-Saharan Africa Average			4.21
Latin America Average			6.04
OECD/BRICS Average			6.43

economic inequality can also be a cause of conflict and of unhappiness. Finally, countries suffering under armed conflict—like Syria, Iraq and Afghanistan—are naturally going to have a lot of unhappy people in them, so we have to take account of such conflicts in the period we're examining.

With all the different factors that bear on happiness levels in a country, we'll want to be able to separate the effect of each one from all the others. That involves looking at the array of observations for all 154 countries in the World Happiness Report, and doing more than 1,200 separate computations. This would have been impossible fifty years ago, but today it can be done with the click of a key on a multiple-regression statistical software program. This is now the canonical way of conducting social science research.

The results are reported in Table 5.4 in the Appendix (with a preceding explanation). And what does it tell us? Countries with major economies—the OECD and BRICS nations—are happier than other countries, and the sub-Saharan nations are considerably less happy. Countries are happier when there's less income inequality, and unhappy when they're beset by major conflicts. Population density doesn't seem to matter, and one reason might be that advances in transportation and communication have shrunk the differences between life in sparsely and densely populated places. Finally, more people equals less happiness. It's what Sherman predicted: bigness is badness.

It's true that the United States is happier than most countries. While not as happy as a group of smaller nations, as measured by the World Happiness Report, it obviously has something going for it. In particular, there are two things that distinguish the United States from the other heavily populated countries, which are generally unhappy.

First, the United States is a federal country, like Canada and Australia, where the central government's power is shared with states or provinces. While it's more centralized than it was a hundred years ago, power is still dispersed across the country, much more than in China or Russia. If we were a unitary country without our state governments, we would effectively be a larger country, and the message from Table 5.4. is that we'd be a less happy country. If we were more decentralized, perhaps we'd be happier still.

Second, America has adopted free-market economics, and that has made it wealthy and one of the world's premier destinations for immigrants. The least happy countries are those that people are leaving in droves, often as refugees, not the ones that people are trying to get into.

If bigness equals badness, there are ways a large country can offset this, such as with federalism and free markets. In addition, the optimal population size is not zero, and there are advantages as well as disadvantages to a large population. It's a question of tradeoffs. Public corruption, national defense, political and personal freedom, and trade and infrastructure costs are all a function of size, so we'll look at each in turn.

6

BIGNESS AND CORRUPTION

If small states are happier than big ones, one reason is that big states are more corrupt. As Montesquieu and Rousseau argued, there's a greater sense of solidarity in smaller states, such as Finland, where people are less diverse and more trusting of each other. They'll feel less helpless and less alienated from their government. Montesquieu was also right in thinking that small countries won't have so many wasteful interest groups as larger ones. In sum, governments will be more attuned to the interests of their citizens in smaller states.

All this matters, because if we're corrupt we pay for it. Corrupt states are poorer than honest ones. And in a large country such as the United States, that's an argument for secession.

There are two kinds of corruption, public and private, and it's only the former that concerns us here. Private corruption is the cheating that goes on between private parties, in businesses or foundations. The privately corrupt might skim off the top, for example, like Moe Green in *The Godfather*. This happens in every country, large and small, and there are laws against it. Country size wouldn't seem to matter. Then there's public corruption, which is the corruption of public officials, legislators, bureaucrats and judges. It could be bribery, or simply the undue influence of lobbyists and interest groups on public policy. The question is whether a greater size contributes to a country's public corruption. And the answer is that it does.

The Cost of Corruption

The United States has a public corruption problem. Many Americans find this hard to believe, so it's helpful to remind them of places like Mississippi, with its crony politicians, or Illinois, where four of the state's last seven governors have gone to prison. For our purposes, however, the comparison that matters is with other countries, and for that we can turn to a German NGO, Transparency International, and its Corruption Perceptions Index (CPI).

The CPI gathers reports from respected local observers on questions such as whether the country's public officials can be bribed, and whether they'll be prosecuted if they are. Has the government been captured by special interests? Are there transparency laws, and what happens to whistleblowers?[1] On this basis, the CPI rates countries on a scale of 1 to 100, from least to most honest. In the 2017 ranking of 180 countries, the United States had a score of 75, putting it in a three-way tie for sixteenth place.

The United States is very wealthy, but we're not as rich as we'd be with less public corruption. That's the message from Figure 6.1, which plots a country's wealth (the 2017 per capita gross domestic product) against its 2016 CPI ranking. Among the 141 countries examined, corrupt and poor Venezuela is in the lower left corner, while honest and rich Luxembourg and Singapore are in the top right corner. The diagonal line represents a statistical regression that captures the relation between wealth and honesty, or between public corruption and poverty.

The model tells us that if America, with a CPI ranking of 75, could move up to Canada's 82, the resulting increase in national wealth would amount to a $6,000 pay raise for every American. It would be a $12,000 increase if we moved to New Zealand's 89. These numbers are merely suggestive, mind you. A model is only a model. What is clear, however, is the simple message that more corruption means more poverty. It means there's less money in our pockets, less money to repair crumbling infrastructure, less money for health care. So we might want to know how America could clean up its act.

TABLE 6.1 TRANSPARENCY INTERNATIONAL'S CORRUPTION PERCEPTIONS INDEX 2017

Country	Rank	Score	Country	Rank	Score
New Zealand	1	89	Netherlands	8	82
Denmark	2	88	United Kingdom	8	82
Finland	3	85	Germany	12	81
Norway	3	85	Australia	13	77
Switzerland	3	85	Hong Kong	13	77
Singapore	6	84	Iceland	13	77
Sweden	6	84	Austria	16	75
Canada	8	82	Belgium	16	75
Luxembourg	8	82	**United States**	16	75

FIGURE 6.1 LESS CORRUPTION, MORE WEALTH

Ordinary Least Squares regression

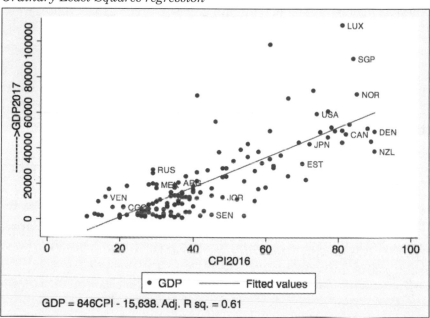

GDP = 846CPI - 15,638. Adj. R sq. = 0.61

Sources: GDP per Capita, CIA; Transparency International Corruption Perceptions Index 2016.

As we'll see, public corruption is the curse of bigness, and America is a big country. But other things contribute to public corruption too, including our campaign finance laws, which are laxer than those of other countries.

Campaign Finance

America's campaign finance laws are a net with the curious feature that the small fish get caught and the big fish sail through. They make criminals of small-donor naïfs while permitting lobbyists and the firms that employ them to navigate around the technicalities. Like every country, we criminalize the bribery of public officials, but we've permitted donors, particularly lobbying firms, to influence elected officials through campaign contributions and through offers to hire them once they leave public office.

Donors expect to have their calls returned and their opinions respected, and that's not a crime. "Ingratiation and access...are not corruption," ruled Justice Anthony Kennedy in *Citizens United*.[2] Then, in a subsequent case, Chief Justice John Roberts took it one step further. Campaign donors can not only gain access, but can expect that the officials they support will respond to their interests. There's nothing wrong with that, said Roberts. Rather, it's "a central feature of democracy."[3]

Roberts was right so far as it concerns ideological donors, such as George Soros or Charles Koch. People or groups that donate to a political party because they want it to win, or more likely because they think the other party is composed of knaves and fools, aren't corrupt. Rather, they're patriots, whichever party they might support.

The same can be said of the donors who have fueled the increase in super PAC spending, which now approaches the $1.5 billion of official party spending in presidential elections.[4] In *Buckley v. Valeo* the Supreme Court held that donors can contribute unlimited dollars to super PACs that do not coordinate with a candidate,[5] and in *Citizens United* the Court held that super PAC ads can ask viewers to vote for or against a candidate, again provided that they don't coordinate with the candidate. That ruling has upset liberal editorialists who don't like competition in telling people how to vote, but the barriers to coordination with a candidate help ensure that super PAC money won't be prompted by a corrupt desire for a return favor from a public official. There's even less reason to worry about pay-for-play corruption when "dark money" is given anonymously under section 501(c)(4) of the Internal Revenue Code. If the gift really is anonymous, the official won't know whom to reward when he is elected.

That kind of money comes from ideological donors, and they aren't the problem. Instead, it's the donors who *do* seek a quid pro quo, America's lobbyists in particular. Lobbyists donated $3.3 billion to campaign chests in 2012,[6] more than all super PAC and presidential campaign giving combined. The result is pay-for-play networks in which lobbyists and their clients are rewarded for their campaign contributions with government favors from public officials. The multitudinous rules they craft serve to shield government largess from the public eye, and have helped create the regulatory state on steroids that Donald Trump called the "swamp," which has been a leading cause of the decline in American economic growth.[7]

Firms that funnel money to candidates through lobbyists are getting their money's worth in the form of tariff protection and tax subsidies, and various other kinds of government assistance. In 2011 the *Economist* reported on a study that created a lobbying index for fifty American firms (lobbying expenditures divided by firm value), and reported that the index had outperformed the S&P 500 by 11 percent a year since 2002.[8] Those firms did well, the national economy less so. Firms that lobby also lower their tax rate, and one study reported that for every dollar a firm spends on targeted tax loopholes the payoff is between six and twenty dollars.[9] In addition, they have a significantly lower probability of being prosecuted for fraud.[10]

Apart from direct contributions, lobbyists can organize fundraising events and serve on fundraising committees for a candidate. There are also gifts in kind, such as polling, mass communication efforts and coalition building. What's even more troubling is the "revolving door" through which lobbying firms hire former congressmen, to take advantage of their contacts in government. About half of the congressmen who leave elective office become lobbyists, and so they'll be extra attentive to the desires of a future employer. After all, a congressman can double, triple or quadruple his salary by going on to work as a lobbyist. In the cynical view of one former representative, Jim Cooper, Congress has become a "farm team" for lobbying firms on Washington's K Street.[11] All of this needs to be banned, along the lines I've suggested elsewhere.[12]

Minoritarian Misbehavior

There's another reason we have a corruption problem: the United States is simply too big. Madison thought bigness meant less corruption, and in 1787 he may have been right. In "Vices of the Political System of the United States," he warned about special interests that bend the public purse in their selfish direction, and he said this would be less common in small states.

One example that Madison had in mind was religious groups. A majority religion or denomination might seek the same public financial support that the Episcopalians had enjoyed in Virginia before the state disestablished religion in 1785. To Jefferson and Madison, religious establishments were a form of corruption, since members of minority religions would have to contribute to the majority religion. But this would be more of a problem in small states than in America as a whole, said Madison. While Episcopalians might be dominant in the South, and Congregationalists in the North, there would not be a national majority religious denomination. All would be minorities, and one minority would check another in the competition for power.

The bigger the country, thought Madison, the less likely that one group would find itself in a majority and be able to oppress minority groups. The concern about *majoritarian misbehavior* was therefore an argument for shifting power from the state governments to a stronger national government. Another form of majoritarian misbehavior that Madison foresaw was in conflicts between different economic classes. He warned of "agrarian reforms" in which a majority of poor landless voters would seize the property of a rich landed minority,[13] as has happened in Zimbabwe.

But there was another possibility for collective misbehavior under a new constitution. The Continental and state bonds issued during the Revolution were deeply discounted in value, and the nation's credit was weak. To place the new country on a sound financial footing, it was thought necessary to redeem the bonds at par. The problem was that many Americans opposed this measure. The bonds had been purchased on the cheap by a few "stock-jobbing" financial arbitrageurs, and the many original purchasers would feel cheated by a bailout. "There was a great distinction," said George Mason, between the original creditors and "those who purchased fraudulently of the ignorant and distressed."[14] Looking back through a Marxist prism, the historian Charles Beard saw the dispute as a class struggle between a rising capitalist class and a feudal agrarian class.[15]

What George Mason and Charles Beard described was not majoritarian misbehavior, but just the opposite: the oppression of a majority of Americans by a concentrated and powerful financial minority. Concern about *minoritarian misbehavior*, the tyranny of a minority or of narrow interest groups, has been a constant in American politics, from George Mason's contempt for stock-jobbers, to the fulminations of nineteenth-century populists such as Andrew Jackson and William Jennings Bryan. In the next century, William Z. Ripley, an economist (and racist), wrote of an economic struggle between wealth creators on Main Street and a smaller group of parasitical Wall Street speculators.[16]

We saw the same clash again in the 2008–9 bank bailout, which was said to have rescued our financial system but led to a jobless economic recovery. Those who defend the bailout tell us it saved the U.S. economy and prevented the Great Recession from turning into another Great Depression. It's hard to argue either for or against that proposition, since we can't know what would have happened otherwise. What can be shown is that the policies of the Federal Reserve and the U.S. government shifted wealth from a large number of dispersed and disorganized losers to a small number of powerful, concentrated winners. The Fed's near-zero interest rates made banks less willing to extend loans, especially to middle-class small businessmen. The low interest rates were also bad news for people, particularly retirees, who looked to interest from government bonds for their income. "In this way," noted Joseph Stiglitz, "there was a large transfer of wealth from the elderly to the government, and from the government to the bankers."[17]

The Communist Manifesto proclaimed that "the history of all hitherto existing society is the history of class struggles." That rather overstates the matter. But the history of America, in its banking and financial laws, its antitrust and tort laws, is importantly the history of minoritarian misbehavior and class struggles. Today we see it when lobbyists send campaign contributions to a politician and then employ their privileged access to shift government favors their way.

The concern about minoritarian misbehavior turns Madison's argument for bigness on its head. In 1787, he was right that special-interest corruption would be more of a problem in small states than in large ones. When travel and communication were so slow, interest groups weren't able organize at the national level. But Madison didn't anticipate how technological improvements and the expansion of the federal government might change both the costs and the benefits of organizing a nationwide interest group. Today it's about as easy to form a national interest group as one at the state level, and there's much more bang for your buck if you're operating from Washington, D.C., rather than Dover, Delaware. Today, the influence of concentrated interest groups at the national level—which is to say minoritarian misbehavior—is a greater concern than majoritarian misbehavior. And that's an argument for smallness, not bigness.

Madison's insight about the difficulty of organizing an interest group remains useful, however. While it doesn't account for the rise of industry groups at the national level, it does explain why we don't see effective consumer groups opposing them. A classic example is the sugar industry, which benefits from tariffs that raise sugar prices 64 to 92 percent above the world average.[18] Poorer Americans spend a greater proportion of their earnings on food, and the higher sugar prices hurt them more than rich Americans. But they're no match for the lobbyists employed by America's sugar producers.

You might wonder why a large number of consumers couldn't organize against the sugar lobby. It comes down to the collective action problem we saw in Chapter 4. If it's costly to organize an interest group, the costs are disproportionately high for dispersed groups. In the case of the sugar tariff, it's 120 sugar producers on one side versus 330 million American consumers on the other side, and it's harder for the dispersed nationwide consumer group to act on a collective basis against the smaller, concentrated group of sugar producers. So Madison did have a point, but he didn't see the whole picture. In a big country, wasteful interest groups like the sugar lobby are easily formed, while benign groups like a consumers' coalition are much harder to organize. Thus we get the minoritarian misbehavior that makes big countries more corrupt.

That's the story we get from Table 6.2 in the Appendix. In a sample of 140 countries in 2017, the more populous countries were significantly more corrupt, even after taking other relevant factors into account. Today, minoritarian misbehavior trumps majoritarian misbehavior, whatever might have been the case in 1787. In addition, with greater total wealth, larger countries have more swag to attract lobbyists and their clients. There are more lobbyists per capita in the United States than in Finland, since the rewards for capturing the government are so much greater here.

In sum, the relation between corruption and bigness is like that between Typhoid and Typhoid Mary. That, in turn, is an argument for secession, when a country is overlarge.

Federalism

Bigger size means more corruption for countries in general, but what about the United States in particular? The most egregious forms of American corruption seem to occur at the state level, in places like Mississippi and Illinois. Federal oversight has helped to police local criminal corruption, and so the lesson about size and corruption is threefold. First, smaller is better, as Table 6.2 in the Appendix shows. Second, if the country is big, federalism is a good idea. Third, in a federal system, the federal government should have the power to police corruption at the state and local level.

The feds can't go after the noncriminal corruption of lobbyists who don't breach campaign finance laws. However, the FBI is very effective in policing criminal corruption such as bribery, more so than the local police. A pay-for-play network can burrow so deeply within a small jurisdiction that it corrupts the local justice system and resists the efforts of local law enforcement to enforce criminal laws. That was the story of Chicago in the 1930s, before the FBI and Eliot Ness put Al Capone in prison. The mobsters had put the touch on the Chicago police, but couldn't buy off Ness's "untouchables."

This isn't to say that the FBI is above reproach. Its agents have permitted their political biases to influence their decisions, and have provided presidents with personal dirt on their enemies. Director J. Edgar Hoover was thought to have insulated himself from the threat of removal by the information the FBI had gathered about the presidents under whom he ostensibly served, and some think this amounted to blackmail. In the fallout from the Mueller investigation of the Trump administration, there's reason to worry that we've seen the same kind of improper behavior by partisan FBI agents. The bureau has also shown an excess of zeal that can border on criminality, and generally hotfoots its cases and excludes honest local police forces. Nevertheless, the bureau is composed of thousands of honest and highly skilled agents who can shine a spotlight on local corruption. It can bring in outsiders who aren't tainted by local pay-for-play networks, and when honest local officials are outmanned it can bring in far more agents, as well as better investigative technology, to put corrupt local officials in jail.

Sometimes corrupt congressmen are convicted, as happened in the Abscam scandal forty years ago. More often, it's state officials who are found to have misbehaved, in places like Mississippi. An empirical study in 2014 looked at federal prosecutions of state officials, and lo, the Magnolia State led all the rest.[19] That's nothing new, and it goes back to Mississippi's racist history and the way in which its legal system collaborated in denying African Americans their rights.

In 1964, local law enforcement in Philadelphia, Mississippi, organized a lynch mob that killed three civil rights workers (one black, two white). When the three were reported missing, the U.S. attorney general, Robert Kennedy, sent hundreds of FBI agents and military to search for them. Their charred station wagon was found the next day, and the remains of the three men were uncovered several weeks later, but only after searchers had come across the remains of eight other missing African Americans. Meanwhile, public outrage spurred the adoption of the federal Civil Rights Act.

A local Mississippi judge subpoenaed the FBI agents investigating the crime to reveal their sources, but the acting U.S. attorney general, Nicholas Katzenbach, refused to allow it. He considered the Mississippi court system so corrupt and tainted with racism that the information would be turned over to the murderers and their lawyers.[20] The case went to the Supreme Court, where Thurgood Marshall, the solicitor general, and John Doar, the assistant attorney general, argued for the prosecution.[21] Standing before the jury, Doar explained why the case was being argued in federal court.

> I am here because your National Government is concerned
> about your local law enforcement....When local law enforcement

officials become involved as participants in violent crime and use their position, power and authority to accomplish this, there is very little to be hoped for, except with assistance from the Federal Government.[22]

What had protected the murderers before the federal government stepped in was Mississippi's crony culture, in which judges hung out with lawyers, officials traded off favors and a code of silence kept people from talking to outsiders. Years later, the same kind of old-boy network, and some of the same players, created Mississippi's corrupt trial lawyer industry, where lawyers schmoozed with and bribed judges. Mississippi's justice system winked at this, and it took the federal government, in the form of the U.S. Attorney's Office and the FBI, to put people in jail.[23]

Would there be more or less corruption, then, if a state or region of America were to secede? If Mississippi seceded, there would be no John Doar to come in from the outside to prosecute corrupt local officials. If all of the old Confederacy left the Union, the size of the federal government, including the federal justice system, would necessarily be smaller, and that would mean less oversight of pockets of local corruption.

Does that make an argument for bigness as a cure for corruption? Yes, if the problem were simply a matter of criminal corruption that the federal Justice Department can prosecute, such as the pay-for-play networks that traffic in bribes. Sometimes, however, corruption is nothing more than a pattern of reciprocal favors to grease the wheels and get deals done, the pay-for-play of the lobbyist's legal campaign contributions. That's not a crime, and federal oversight is powerless in such cases.

A useful example of this kind of corruption occurred in 2008, when the governor of Illinois, Rod Blagojevich, had the right to appoint someone to the Senate to fill the remainder of Barack Obama's term. "Blago" told Obama: I'll pick someone you like; just give me a seat in the cabinet in return. But Obama turned him down. Upon receiving the news from his chief of staff, Blago said, "They're not willing to give me anything except appreciation. F*** them!"[24]

Sadly for Blagojevich, everything he said was being recorded by the FBI. He was indicted for the attempted sale of a Senate seat, among other offenses, and was sentenced to fourteen years in jail. The U.S. Court of Appeals for the Seventh Circuit reversed on one charge, where the issue was whether the offer of an appointment to the Senate in exchange for a cabinet seat was a criminal offense. It wasn't, the court held. It was merely logrolling, and that was how Earl Warren came to be appointed chief justice of the United States in exchange for delivering the California delegation to Eisenhower at the 1952 Republican convention. And any theory of criminal law that made felons of Warren and Eisenhower just wasn't going to wash.

The federal justice system and the FBI can police criminal corruption, but the noncriminal kind of corruption is another thing. Criminal corruption is ordinarily chump change, like the $90,000 found in the freezer of William Jefferson (D-LA) in 2005. By comparison, the legal pay-for-play networks have created what the historian J.G.A. Pocock called "the greatest empire of patronage and influence the world has known."[25] And that form of corruption is much more costly.

Again we're looking at tradeoffs. If a state seceded from the United States, its citizens would lose the benefit of the federal government's oversight of local criminal corruption. On the other hand, being smaller, the seceding state would be less affected by noncriminal corruption and the curse of bigness seen in Table 6.2. There would be fewer dollars in play, and a smaller set of interest groups and lobbyists diverting public dollars to their private ends through legal means. And it's the noncriminal corruption that's ordinarily more troubling.

A bigger state is a more corrupt state, but it helps to divide up the responsibilities for dealing with criminal corruption, as federal countries are able to do. America's justice system is far from perfect, and it's also a messy system in which federal offenses overlap with state ones, as they did when the FBI went after the murderers of the civil rights workers in 1964. But the overlap has permitted the federal government to prosecute criminally corrupt local officials, and this has served to make America less corrupt than it otherwise would be.

7

BIGNESS AND THE MILITARY

America's neoconservatives take pride in our role as the world's policeman. That might be good for the world, but is it good for us? The Iraq war that neoconservatives supported was repudiated in 2006 and again in 2016 by voters who didn't care for nation building abroad when they thought their own country was ailing. They wanted us to intervene less often in the affairs of other countries. If we were a smaller country, we would necessarily have more modest foreign policy goals and might spend less on our military per capita.

Bigness does have its advantages, since greater size offers protection from attack. André the Giant didn't worry about muggers the way 97-pound weaklings do. And what's true of people is true of countries too. Think of how its geographical size protected Russia, how Napoleon was drawn deep into it and how his Grand Army was destroyed in its retreat. At the same time, their very size and wealth tempt big countries to throw their weight around, to dominate their regions or even the world, and this can be seen as a cost of bigness. So we'd want to find the ideal position on the scale between a too-small and fragile Finland at one end and a too-big, imperialistic France at the other.

Bigness and Self-Defense

At the 1787 Constitutional Convention, the Framers debated whether the thirteen states would need a stronger union for purposes of self-defense. The first defect in the Articles of Confederation that Madison's Virginia Plan mentioned was the lack of protection against foreign invasion.[1] Madison worried that states would make treaties with other countries and then breach them, which "must involve us in the calamities of foreign wars."[2] Hamilton too warned that states would enter into alliances with foreign powers and entangle themselves in foreign wars.[3] The same arguments were repeated in the first numbers of *The Federalist Papers*, written by John Jay.

None of this much impressed the other delegates, however. Many spoke openly about the possibility of disunion, with a candor that would shock anyone who assumes it was inevitable that the delegates would agree on a constitution. Some wondered if we would even need a strong military when our isolation would keep us at peace. That's what George Washington would say in his Farewell Address in 1796.

> Europe has a set of primary interests which to us have none; or
> a very remote relation. Hence she must be engaged in frequent
> controversies, the causes of which are essentially foreign to
> our concerns.... Our detached and distant situation invites and
> enables us to pursue a different course.... Why forego the advan-
> tages of so peculiar a situation?

Even Madison, in *Federalist* 41, saw the advantage in America's geographic isolation, like that of Great Britain. Just as its separation from the Continent had saved Britain from the need for a strong army and the danger of military rule, the same happy condition could be expected for America.

Was there anything like a threat from America's neighbors? In 1790, Canada had a population of about 200,000 people, which was one-twentieth that of the United States. It was not a rival of any kind except in the production of beaver pelts and maple syrup. Until the Jay Treaty of 1795, the British continued to hold the western forts in territory that had been ceded to the United States by the 1783 Treaty of Paris, but this was in the nature of a mechanic's lien for the American failure to observe its treaty obligations to the Loyalists and British creditors, rather than a real military threat.

As Washington would have wished, America's military remained small until the Civil War. During the War of 1812 it totaled fewer than 100,000 men, and it was not much larger during the Mexican-American War. In December 1860 there were only 16,000 people in the military, many of whom would join the Confederate forces. By the end of the war, more than two million men had enlisted in the Union army, and another million in the Confederate army. The military then fell to under 100,000 men by the start of the Spanish-American War.

Today we have an armed force of two million and a military budget that exceeds those of the next seven countries combined. In 2017, global military spending was $1,739 billion, and $609 billion of that, or 35 percent, was spent by the United States. In the 2018 Defense Authorization, U.S. military spending was increased to $717 billion, which was 3.8 percent of GDP. When America saw itself threatened by an expansionist Soviet Union, military spending was proportionately higher: 8.4 percent of GDP in 1960.[4] The fall of communism brought a "peace dividend," and American military spending fell from 5.7 percent of GDP in 1991 to 2.9 percent in 2001. With 9/11 and the Iraq war it rose again, to 4.7 percent in 2010. Under the 2019 budget it's 3.6 percent.

The numbers have changed, and so has the need for a huge military. Since 1991, America has dominated a unipolar world. It is no longer threatened by the Soviets, and its reach extends to every corner of the globe. No empire in the past —not the Roman Empire, not the Napoleonic empire can compare

How did this happen? How did America abandon its happy isolation to become the world's dominant military power, with an empire of influence and strength of a kind never before seen in world history? There are three possible answers: interest-group corruption, a presidential constitution and the country's bigness.

The Military-Industrial Complex

The first explanation is the form of interest-group corruption that President Eisenhower called the "military-industrial complex" in his Farewell Address.[5] He warned against a defense industry that teams up with the military to shape policy decisions about spending and diplomacy. As if to evidence this, defense industry stock prices fell when Trump signaled that a meeting with North Korea's President Kim had been a success.[6]

By itself, the influence of the defense industry doesn't explain why we spend more per capita on our military than other countries. Every First World country has a military-industrial complex, and if our defense industry is bigger, the reason might be that our military and our defense budget are bigger. We have a military budget of over $600 billion, and about half of this is awarded to defense contractors. Like bears to honey, lobbyists are drawn to that money.

The size of our defense industry is arguably not just a consequence of a large military, since causation can also work in the other direction. We might have a large military because of how the defense industry can influence legislators in their appropriation decisions. And that is because of our relatively lax campaign finance laws.

There are anywhere from seven hundred to a thousand defense lobbyists in the United States, almost twice the number of congressmen, and many of the lobbyists are former congressmen who went through the revolving door.[7] Defense contractors outspend other industries in corporate donations to political action committees.[8] Between 2009 and 2017 they spent more than $1 billion on lobbying, and all in all it looks like money well spent. This is plausibly one explanation for the size of our military.

The Constitution

Another possible explanation for a bloated American military is the infirmities of a presidential form of government, as compared with a parliamentary system. An American president has a largely unfettered power to take the country to war, as well as the incentive to do so in order to boost his popularity. This in turn can result in higher military expenditures.

Empirical studies report that presidents embark on war to divert attention from unpopular domestic affairs.[9] One example might be the cruise missile strikes in Afghanistan and Sudan that President Bill Clinton ordered in August 1998, precisely when Monica Lewinsky was giving testimony before a grand jury. The targeted sites were believed to be connected with Osama bin Laden's terror network, and the strikes came two weeks after bombings of two U.S. embassies. But the public noticed a similarity to the plot of *Wag the Dog*, a film released several months earlier, portraying a president who launches a war to distract attention from a sex scandal.

Prime ministers in parliamentary countries have similar powers to launch a war, but they are also subjected to oversight of a kind from which American presidents are shielded by the separation of powers. A robust parliamentary debate is likely to expose facts behind a manufactured crisis, such as the 1964 Gulf of Tonkin incident that was used to justify the American buildup of forces in Vietnam, while many of those facts remain hidden in a less transparent presidential regime. This could explain why I've found that presidential countries spend more on their militaries than parliamentary ones as a percentage of GDP.[10]

Couldn't Congress come to the rescue, and rein in a militaristic president? Congressional support is required for a declaration of war, after all, but the last time war was declared was the day after the attack on Pearl Harbor. Needless to say, it wasn't the last time that American forces were sent into battle. Congress also has the power of the purse and the ability to defund a foreign war. But the last time it attempted to do so when American troops were at risk was during the War of 1812, and the antiwar Federalist Party never recovered from the shame of failing to support our troops. We don't like to deny our boys the resources they need when their lives are on the line, and even Barack Obama as a senator found it prudent to vote supplies during the Iraq insurgency.

For these reasons, America's presidential system of government has plausibly served to make it more militaristic, with higher levels of military spending than parliamentary countries. But if we want a parliamentary regime, we're 233 years too late.

Bigness and Glory

There is a third explanation why America and other large countries spend so much on their militaries, and it's one rooted in the *animus dominandi*, the desire to dominate. We see it in the urge to show superiority in the classroom and on the sports field, and in a country's military spending. And it's the bigger countries that want to ride in triumph through Persepolis. Smaller countries don't have that option.

This explains the puzzling fact that bigger (more populous) countries spend more on their militaries than small countries, as a percentage of GDP, even though their very size insulates bigger countries from danger, as both Napoleon and Hitler discovered when they attacked Russia. Bigness also results in economies of scale. It should be cheaper for one large country to equip and maintain a million-man army than for ten smaller countries to do the same for ten separate armies of 100,000 each. For these reasons, we might expect smaller countries to spend more to defend themselves than larger countries. But it's just the opposite, and America in particular has an oversized military.

Bigger countries like to throw their weight around. That's what the empirical study reported in Table 7.2 in the Appendix suggests.[11] For all regressions, a larger population is significantly correlated with higher military expenditure as a percentage of GDP. The level of military spending even seems unrelated to actual conflicts. What determines the level of military spending more than anything else is simply size: more people, more military spending.

Table 7.1 lists the top ten military spenders, and only three of them might be thought to need a strong military for defensive reasons: Saudi Arabia, Japan and South Korea. China is threatened by no one, but threatens other countries with its military buildup. As a percentage of GDP, its spending does not seem excessive, but the figure is disputed and does not include the military bases that China has created on artificial islands hundreds of miles from its shores, projecting its military might deep into Oceana.[12] It has deployed anti-ship surface-to-air missiles and even nuclear-capable bombers in the middle of the most heavily traveled sea-lanes, leading to fears that China seeks to dictate the terms of navigation to the world and dominate the entire Southeast Asia region.[13] China also sees its trade and energy links, such as its "Belt and Road" initiative with its railroad and pipeline spending in Asia, as a method of expanding its strategic power as well as its economic clout.

Russian military spending as a percentage of GDP is relatively high. Vladimir Putin has described the breakup of the Soviet Union

TABLE 7.1 MILITARY EXPENDITURES, TOP TEN COUNTRIES 2017

Country	Military Spending (000s)	Military Spending as a percentage of GDP
United States	609,758	3.1
China	228,231	1.9
Saudi Arabia	69,413	10.3
Russia	66,335	4.3
India	63,924	2.5
France	57,770	2.3
United Kingdom	47,193	1.8
Japan	45,387	0.9
Germany	44,329	1.2
South Korea	39,153	2.6

Source: Stockholm International Peace Research Institute Military Expenditure Database, accessed June 25, 2018.

as the greatest geopolitical tragedy of the twentieth century, and with Russia's wars against Georgia and Ukraine he's made a start at reversing it. He also has extended Russia's sphere of influence to the former Soviet states in Asia, and has made his country a dominant player in Middle East conflicts. As with China, this is a matter of projecting Russian might beyond its borders, and not of self-defense.

Then there's us. After the Second World War, when an exhausted Britain passed on the torch, we became the world's policeman. We're responsible for 35 percent of the world's military spending, more than China, Russia and the next five countries combined. In doing so, we have created a global commons, with all the wealth gains that come from international commerce, open sea-lanes, unhindered trade and a U.S. dollar that's the world's reserve currency. Because of us, world GDP has increased twentyfold since the Second World War, and so we're now hearing American demands to make our allies pay their fair share of defense spending.

President Trump's criticism of our free-riding NATO allies, backed up by his trade threats, seems to be having an effect. Allies are slowly increasing their military spending, but they would never match ours unless we cut our spending down to their levels and gave up our role as the world's policeman. Call it "Atlas Shrugged." But it's not going to happen, for two reasons. First, if the global commons shrank, the

United States would be a big loser too, maybe the biggest. Second, like other large countries, America seeks to project its power for the glory it brings.

Glory is a discredited word, one that might conjure up the Knights of the Round Table. But it's the most universal goal of mankind. You can see it even in ordinary conversation, where the quick-witted dictate the subject and squelch intruders. Dr. Johnson dominated the conversation in company with Burke, Goldsmith and Sheridan, but one day a visitor sought to interrupt him. Scarce able to stop the flow of words, the visitor then stamped his feet. Johnson asked him, "Why do you stamp, Sir?" The stranger responded, "Because you stamped, and I was resolved not to give you the advantage of a stamp in the argument." Ah, sighed Edith Sitwell, there were giants in those days![14]

There is a sense that the glorious deserve their renown, and that glory bears a badge of honor. And of all the different kinds of glory—celluloid, mathematical, culinary—none shines brighter than military glory. Even the humblest citizens sense that they share in it. The East Ender in Kipling's day might think that, poor as he was, at least he partook of membership in the British Empire. It is the same for Americans today who bask in the glory of their country.

Nietzsche thought it natural that we should seek power and that the weak should serve the strong.[15] Realist students of international relations, such as Hans J. Morgenthau, agreed and identified a Nietzschean desire for dominance as the principal cause of rivalry and conflict between nations.[16] Once a country finds itself able to become top dog, it will have difficulty resisting the temptation to do so. History is replete with stories of small states—Athens, Macedon, Rome—that rose to greatness when the opportunity presented itself, but shows few that turned their back on conquest, like Sparta or China under the Ming dynasty, when they had the chance to expand.

Military glory comes with a cost, however. First, more armed conflict results in more military deaths. The second Iraq war, from 2003 to 2011, cost the lives of 4,424 American soldiers. There were 179 British military fatalities and 139 from other coalition partners. Canada stayed out of the conflict and there were no Canadian deaths.

A bigger military also means a heavier tax burden. In fact, we won our independence in no small part because the British lost their appetite for the war and the intolerable financial burden it imposed. The government was forced to increase taxation to meet the expenses of the campaign, and the House of Commons was bombarded with petitions to cut government spending. As much as its military defeats, this explains why Britain agreed to American independence.

The costs of a large military, in money and in lives, might be acceptable if you like a strong military for its own sake, and regional or world dominance. So then you might favor a large country with a huge population. But if you're not sure that military glory is worth the cost, you might prefer a small state, with a modest military budget. And that might be an argument for secession. Imagine what the last fifty years of history would have looked like if America had been split into two or three different countries. There would likely have been no Vietnam War, and almost certainly no second Iraq war.

What would secession mean for California in this regard? Of the U.S. military budget of $693 billion for FY 2019, California taxpayers provided one-eighth, or $87 billion. Suppose that the new Republic of California took its military budget down to Canadian levels, as a percentage of GDP. That would allow for a peace dividend of about $1,100 for each Californian. But why have a military at all? Why not save the entire $87 billion? That would amount to a $1,900 peace dividend for each Californian.

Perhaps California might prefer to invest the moneys saved in its social programs. It's often been said that other countries finance their single-payer medical systems by free-riding on the America military. If California saved the $87 billion a year it now puts into military spending, that would almost pay for a single payer system, according to estimates made by the *Los Angeles Times*.[17] Suppose, then, that Californians were offered this choice in a secession referendum: You can stay in the Union and fund the American military, or you can leave it and fund health care for all Californians. Given the state's liberal politics, it's tempting to think one knows how that referendum would come out.

Or perhaps not. What California secessionists would be giving up is a share in the glory of belonging to the greatest power on earth.

8

BIGNESS AND FREEDOM

Is bigness a threat to freedom? To answer the question, we first need to define what we mean by freedom. I've had intelligent people tell me that Britain can't be free because its laws are too tough on libelers. In France, officious gendarmes demand "papers, please," and we take pride that this doesn't happen here. But people in other countries wonder whether the United States is really free when there are so many criminal offenses and so many people in jail. Evidently there are many different ways of understanding freedom, and chauvinists are apt to praise their own country's freedoms while condemning the mote in the other country's eye. Between First World countries, this is mostly what Freud called the narcissism of petty differences. But in the most widely accepted ranking of freedom, smaller countries are freer than big ones.

Freedom for Whom?

It's not always easy to say what freedom means, but we can begin by noting that real-world freedoms in practice are what matter, not abstract rights on paper. During most of its history, America's admirably liberal set of constitutional rights coexisted with the harshest restrictions on people of the wrong color. Before the Thirteenth

89

Amendment they were slaves, and for a hundred years thereafter they labored under the most severe legal disabilities that a country could inflict upon its citizens. Over that period, America was less than fully free. But it was far freer than the USSR, notwithstanding all the freedoms of speech and the press guaranteed under the Soviet Constitution. Abstract rights aren't much good when they're merely paper rights, or when they're denied to a portion of the population.

We can be happy that the civil rights revolution has lifted America above its troubled past, making it a beacon of freedom for the world. Individually, we enjoy a well-protected set of personal liberties, the freedom to speak our mind and practice our religion, as well as the economic freedom to hold property and start a business. We also enjoy a strong set of political rights that come with living in a democratic society where government officials must campaign for our votes.

We used to think that personal and political freedoms went together, like horse and carriage. This was called the "Washington Consensus." When a state liberalized its economy it would create a middle class that would demand political freedom. That seemed to be what had happened in Chile, when the free-market Pinochet regime was followed by a liberal democracy. Insofar as this pattern was spreading around the globe, it represented what Francis Fukuyama called "the end of history," the point where the big questions of politics have been settled. The best possible kind of state is one with a free-market economy and guarantees of personal and political liberty.[1] That's as good as it gets.

But now China presents us with a rival model, a "Beijing Consensus," granting its people economic freedoms while denying them political liberty. "We'll make you rich," says the government. "Just don't bother asking for democracy." Or for too many other personal freedoms. The lack of political freedom matters, however, and in time it may prove to be China's undoing. But for the moment, the Chinese government has made its people freer by making them richer. Over the last thirty years, the number of Chinese people living in extreme poverty (on less than $1.25 a day) fell from 84 to 12 percent of the population, from 835 to 156 million, an expansion of wealth unmatched in history.[2] As a consequence, freedom expanded, for one thing that freedom means is having choices. Today we often see Chinese tourists spending money in America. We didn't see this forty years ago. This means that the

Chinese are freer today, even though they lack political freedoms or the personal freedoms we take for granted.

Laws can either guarantee or restrict our freedom, whether personal or political, and we can also be hemmed in by social norms. People can be legally free and yet handcuffed by social disapproval. In Victorian England, John Stuart Mill called this the dreaded censorship of social custom, and in today's America too there are things that cannot be said, ideas that cannot be expressed. Sometimes that's for the good, sometimes not. In either case it explains why many Europeans, from Stendhal in the nineteenth century to Stephen Fry today, have thought America less free than France or England.

The way in which the received ideas of the day constrain what is permissible to express was something George Orwell saw when he warned against Soviet communism after the Second World War. Four publishers turned down *Animal Farm*, in one case after the British Ministry of Information objected that the Soviets might take offense since they were so clearly the book's target. It simply wouldn't do to upset them. And so Orwell wrote a preface to the book, on the theme of self-censorship, but it was never published with the book until many years later, after it had been published by the *Times Literary Supplement* in 1972. In the preface Orwell wrote:

> At any given moment there is an orthodoxy, a body of ideas which it is assumed that all right-thinking people will accept without question. It is not exactly forbidden to say this, that or the other, but it is "not done" to say it, just as in mid-Victorian times it was "not done" to mention trousers in the presence of a lady. Anyone who challenges the prevailing orthodoxy finds himself silenced with surprising effectiveness. A genuinely unfashionable opinion is almost never given a fair hearing, either in the popular press or in the highbrow periodicals.[3]

We're seeing similar complaints about the way in which today's social media giants—Google, Facebook, Twitter—suppress conservative voices. Some right-wing links seem to disappear quickly on Google, leading conservatives to try other search engines. Twitter has banned some conservative provocateurs and "shadowbanned" others by suppressing their tweets. In response, there are calls to apply antitrust laws and break up the social media giants as natural monopolies. That's probably a bad idea, since asking self-interested politicians to promote free speech by silencing people they don't like is probably self-defeating. They're the last people to be trusted to guarantee impartiality. And even if conservatives started their own social media platform, they would probably want to ban voices they consider beyond the pale, such as racist groups.

Our idea of freedom will necessarily be a little subjective. That's what Montesquieu thought, when he defined freedom as "that tranquility of spirit which comes from the opinion each one has of his security."[4] And whether we're tranquil will depend on whose ox is gored. The American Civil Liberties Union used to be led by First Amendment absolutists who, in the name of freedom, defended the right of neo-Nazis to march in Jewish neighborhoods. Today, however, the ACLU is having second thoughts about speech that offends other people. Similarly, if a baker refuses to decorate a wedding cake for a same-sex couple, is he simply exercising his freedom of religion, or cruelly interfering with the couple's freedom of association? "O Liberty! What crimes are committed in thy name!" exclaimed Mme Roland. And what confusion follows when opposing sides both claim it for themselves.

Measuring Freedom

With all the ambiguities surrounding the idea of freedom, we can still measure countries according to how free their people are, both personally and politically, and the most widely used ranking is Freedom House's index of liberal democracies.[5] Freedom House is an NGO based in Washington, D.C., with a deep bench of experts across the world. It relies on teams of regional lawyers, businessmen and scholars for an annual assessment of 195 countries on how well they protect personal and political liberties. The ratings for political freedom are based on questions such as whether there are free and fair elections, with competitive political parties, and whether minority groups are excluded from the political process. The questions on personal or civil liberties focus on freedom of expression and belief, the right of association, the rule of law and personal autonomy.

That's not to say that the Freedom House rankings are free from

FIGURE 8.1 MORE FREEDOM, MORE HAPPINESS

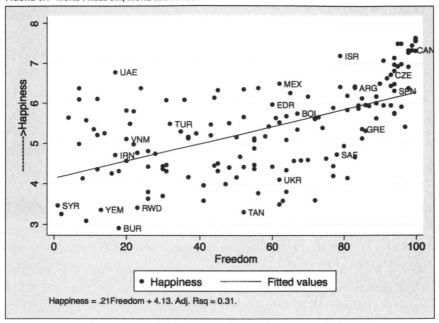

Happiness = .21 Freedom + 4.13. Adj. Rsq = 0.31.

bias. The 2018 report downgrades the United States on political rights "due to growing evidence of Russian interference in the 2016 elections, violations of basic ethical standards by the new administration, and a reduction in government transparency." Freedom House now has the United States tied with Brazil and Argentina in its ranking on political freedom. That might be how many American liberals see things, but it's so over-the-top that it asks to be ignored.

For other countries, however, the Freedom House ratings seem reasonably reliable. So let's see how they might be related to the happiness levels we saw back in Chapter 4, as reported by the World Happiness Report's SWB ratings for 153 countries. The relation is represented in Figure 8.1, and the message is that the free countries of the First World are happy, while unfree countries—like Burundi, Yemen and Syria—are deeply unhappy.

Bigness and Freedom

If we're on the side of happiness, that means we're also on the side of freedom, and the next question is what makes people free or unfree. We'll want to look at a number of factors in addition to a country's size. As I found in *The Once and Future King*, presidential countries are less free than parliamentary ones, so we'll distinguish between systems of government. Another factor to take into account is the ethnic diversity in a country, since a high degree of diversity can produce the kinds of squabbles in which minority rights are restricted, and in extreme cases it can result in civil war, as in Nigeria or Iraq, which clearly threatens freedom. When these factors are separated out, along with regional variables, the story that emerges from Table 7.1 in the Appendix is that smaller, less populous countries are freer than larger countries.

That is what Montesquieu and Rousseau said. Both thought that smaller countries would be freer because public officials would be more responsive to their citizens.[6] One reason is the informational problem that officials face in determining what people want. That's hard enough to do in a city of 100,000 residents, as I've seen in going to city hall with a few other decent, public-minded citizens to take on the Lycra-clad thugs of the bicycle lobby who demand more bike lanes. Moving from the city level to an entire state or country and trying to aggregate what people want will be many times more difficult. At the national level, the number of parties at the table and the number of issues upon it increase exponentially.

The informational problem cuts both ways, too. Our officials won't know what we want, and we won't know much about what they're doing. That's why Hume and Madison proposed a "filtering" process for elections, in which lower-level officers would elect higher-level ones. The informational problem was also Aristotle's argument against bigness.[7] When a state is overlarge, we won't know much about the character of the public officials we choose to rule us. We won't be able to monitor them to find out what deals they cut, how they pressure bureaucrats or even how they vote. And the bigger the state, the greater the problem.

In addition, as countries become larger in population, they'll often become more ethnically, linguistically and religiously diverse, and less likely to have a common set of preferences and sense of identity. People will then be less likely to trust each other and more accepting of side deals crafted by their own interest groups. In low-trust countries there is less willingness to cooperate on the provision of public goods, such as schools and infrastructure. Governments will also be less able to protect property rights and the rule of law, and keep spending down.[8]

It used to be assumed that competition between interest groups in national politics would somehow lead to policies that are the best overall for everyone. The labor unions, the Chamber of Commerce, the churches, the ethnic groups, the sugar lobby and the consumer groups would all clamor to make their voices heard, and all would be balanced to arrive at the greatest good for the greatest number. This was called "pluralism," but it lived in a swamp of pay-for-play corruption, and today you'd be hard pressed to find anyone who believes in it. From the right, it's dismissed by public choice economists who assume that politicians are self-interested and less than enamored with the public good. From the left, the sunnier ways of pluralism did not survive the rise of identity politics and the darker and more thrilling search for Enemies of the People.

If the problem of bigness arises because voters are so distant from public officials, might we bring the government closer to the people by enlarging the House of Representatives? With 435 members in the House, each represents 750,000 people, and it's difficult for an individual representative to get much of a sense of what voters want. The country was much smaller in 1787, and the initial plan was for a ratio of one representative for 40,000 people. On the last day of the Constitutional Convention, George Washington proposed a ratio of one representative for 30,000 people, and this was adopted unanimously.[9] Whether Washington thought it was a point of great importance has been doubted, however. As president of the convention he rarely spoke, and his last-minute interjection was more likely meant to signal that he supported the proposed constitution. In any event, it resulted in a first Congress with only 65 representatives.

What if we returned to the same ratio for today's House of Representatives? If we had one representative for 30,000 people, each representative might know more about his constituents, but the House would consist of 11,000 representatives. No one member would wield any real power, and the House as a whole would be disorganized and unable to coordinate on a course of action. Because a strong government is needed in a large state, an overly powerful executive would emerge to fill the void. He would be a unitary voice, able to act swiftly and propose a single course of action. His power would not be constrained by the legislature, and he would rule as what George Mason called an "elective monarch." This is why Rousseau said that bigger countries are necessarily unfree.[10]

If bigness invites rule by a dictator, dictators also like bigness. With greater size comes grander palaces and more power to push neighbors around. The Winter Palace and Versailles weren't built by democratic rulers. In a world of dictators, countries are overlarge and overcentralized, noted Alberto Alesina, and therefore "democratization and secessions should go hand in hand."[11]

Secession would likely result in a government that is more representative, more attuned to the wishes of the constituents. But that would depend on the size of the seceding state. California has a population of 40 million people, more than most countries have. There are 80 seats in the California State Assembly, with one representative for 500,000 people, which is not much better than the federal ratio. Perhaps the state should be split into three, as some have proposed. By comparison, the South Carolina General Assembly has 170 members, one for every 30,000 people, just as George Washington would have wished. But in either case, secession would serve to bring the government closer to the people, and in so doing it would make people freer.

9

BIGNESS AND WEALTH

U p to now, everything we've seen tells us that small is beautiful. But there are advantages to bigness when it comes to
what makes a country wealthy. So it's a matter of weighing
the benefits of bigness against the costs. If there were only costs, the
optimal size of a country would be vanishingly small. If there were only
benefits, we'd want a one-world government. The trick is finding the
optimal place in between. It's the Goldilocks principle: not too hot, not
too cold, but just right.

What are the benefits of size? If you want your country to be rich,
there are three major advantages to bigness:

- Bigness means an expanded *free-trade zone*, so long as there
  are no internal trade barriers.
- A large country is apt to be better *diversified*, in the sense that
  its economy isn't dependent on a small number of firms.
- Bigger countries can exploit *economies of scale* in their pur-
  chases of goods and services.

There are further economic arguments for a country to remain
large rather than breaking up when we look at the costs of a secession
option, even when it isn't exercised:

- The opt-out remedy of secession gives rise to *underinvestment* costs when the federal government declines to exploit valuable long-term projects whose financing would be threatened by secession.
- A right to secession would encourage piggish *post-constitutional opportunism*, in the form of demands for unwarranted favors from states threatening to leave the Union.
- Negotiations over secession would themselves impose *transaction costs*, by focusing attention on a constitutional crisis and diverting attention from things the government might otherwise usefully do.
- The exit option of secession deprives those who remain of the useful contributions to the debate, or the *voice*, of those who secede.

First we'll examine the economic benefits of bigness, so we can weigh them against the advantages of smallness seen earlier.

Free Trade

With all the disadvantages of bigness, the country's size has given America one of the largest free-trade zones in the world: the United States of America. In economic size, the European Union is bigger today, but only by a bit, and until recently there was nothing comparable to the American free-trade zone.

When the Framers convened in Philadelphia, the problem of interstate trade barriers under the Articles of Confederation was a central issue. The states had levied tariffs on goods passing through to other states, and one delegate asserted that New York could pay the requisitions by the national Congress only because it was "plundering" New Jersey and Connecticut in that way.[1] It is difficult to imagine America's rise to economic greatness had those trade barriers remained in place.

The country's bigness explains why the twentieth century belonged to the United States. Other explanations have been advanced, for example by Claudia Goldin and Lawrence F. Katz, who say that the United States dominated what they call the "human capital" century because it had invested in public education, unlike many of the countries in Europe.[2] National wealth is a function of an educated citizenry, so better schools made for a richer country. But other countries such as Canada and Australia had made comparable investments in their schools. What they lacked was America's population and the extent of its markets. In the nineteenth century, America had doubled in size, and in the next century the country's expanded markets made it rich.

Small countries might capture the benefits of bigness through free-trade agreements with other countries, as Europeans did by creating the Common Market and later the European Union. At present, almost a third of the world's international trade passes relatively free of border duties among the countries of the EU and the parties to NAFTA, and other countries also benefit from free-trade agreements. Antifederalist critics of an overcentralized America argue that the states might have negotiated their own free-trade agreements while remaining under the Articles of Confederation. That would certainly have been a possibility, but it's at least as likely that the trade walls would have stayed up, and that local Trump-like leaders would complain of jobs being shipped to other states.

If a state were to secede today, it might be giving up the benefits of free trade with the rest of the United States, and that would make it poorer. A seceding state might therefore want to have its cake and eat it too, with a free-trade zone that survives the breakup. It's what Quebec separatists called "sovereignty-association," meaning sovereignty without disrupting the province's economic ties with the rest of Canada.

A compromise along those lines is easier said than done, however. Secession is apt to get people riled up, both in the seceding state and in the remaining ones. That's what happened in Canada, when people decided they were sick and tired of hearing about secession, and out of spite voted down a mild constitutional accord that might have satisfied Quebec. In response, Quebeckers elected a separatist government that held a referendum on secession, which very nearly succeeded.

We might not want to fight a civil war over secession, but that's not to say it would be all sweetness and light. Some protectionists might think that if international trade wars are a good idea, why not a trade war within the former United States? The Calexit movement tells its voters that the rest of America hates them, and asks that the state invest in California first. That sounds very much like Donald Trump complaining about Canadians. Would a seceding state even want free trade with the rest of America?

Diversification

We're all familiar with the admonition not to put all of our eggs in one basket. We'll not want to tie up all of our retirement funds in the shares of a single company, not when a well-diversified portfolio of investments in a group of companies promises a like return without the same downside risk. All you need do is hold shares in twenty-odd major industries. Or just invest in a mutual fund.

What's true of individuals is true of nations as well. You wouldn't want your country to depend too closely on the fortunes of a single firm when you depend on the country's solvency to provide you with policing, health care and social security. And that's more likely to be a problem in a small country such as Finland, whose economy was so dependent on Nokia before that company collapsed. In a larger and more diversified Canada, the decline of Blackberry was little more than a hiccup.

When a single industry can take a country down and threaten its safety net, small isn't always beautiful. Take Iceland, for example, with a population of only 350,000. It's also geographically isolated, as islands generally are, and while it's not West Virginia, the possibility of consanguinity among Icelanders is so great that there's an app for seeing to whom you're related before you unwittingly date your cousin. Iceland is so small that when it thought of dollarizing its currency with Canadian currency, withdrawing as little as Can$200,000 from a Toronto ATM would have done the trick. The country relies on a small number of banks, and when they failed in 2008 the country defaulted on its loans and its government collapsed. The stock market declined by 95 percent and almost every Icelandic business went bankrupt.

Americans also suffered through the Great Recession of 2008–9, but we're a bigger country with a more diversified economy, so the whole thing didn't come crashing down. There's something to be said for bigness, then. No one industry is going to take us under. While investors can diversify away the risk of a single firm's default by having a portfolio of twenty firms in their investment basket, the citizens of a small country can't collect more citizenships to manage the risks that come with an undiversified economy. So that's one downside of being an Icelander.

Economies of Scale

Large countries benefit from economies of scale in spending decisions. Things can be done more cost-effectively on a larger scale, whether it's manufacturing a product or building infrastructure. On closer analysis, however, it's not clear whether economies of scale always make the case for bigness.

A country like the United States will spend more on highways than Luxembourg, just because it's bigger. About 3,800 times bigger in area. But what America spends on highways will be less than 3,800 times what Luxembourg spends. That's because a larger country can economize on infrastructure spending, just as a growing business firm can lower its costs of unit production by increasing its output. That's what happened with the great firms of the early twentieth century, such as U.S. Steel, Ford Motors and Exxon. They did one thing very well, and economies of scale allowed them to do it very profitably.

But is that what a modern state is like? Large countries in the modern era are more like the conglomerates that were created in the go-go years of the 1960s, when companies grew by mergers and acquisitions with firms in unrelated industries. All of a sudden, Guns Inc. started producing butter, and War Ltd. began to manufacture ploughshares. It's what Michael Corleone wanted to do in *The Godfather*, when he thought he could leave the rackets for a legitimate business in Las Vegas.

It was called conglomerization, and it sacrificed the economies of scale associated with sticking to one product. Financial experts came up with a number of arguments why this would increase firm value. There would be fewer and better managers running the corporate behemoth, it was claimed, and investors could be fooled with funny accounting tricks. But it was all smoke and mirrors. And if expansion across different industries was always a good thing, where was the stopping point? Why not one big firm that owned everything, Soviet style? At any rate, the house of cards came tumbling down with the breakup and divestiture movement of the 1980s, when managers realized that conglomerates were worth more when split apart.

When all the evidence was in, we saw that the vaunted managerial synergies of combination with firms in unrelated areas were a cost, not a benefit. Managers of a firm in one industry simply didn't have a clue how to run a business in another industry. They would carry their old ways with them, as Michael Corleone did in Las Vegas. I saw this when I was in law practice. One of my firm's clients was an old Anglo-Canadian tobacco company that went on a buying spree for other firms. It realized that tobacco was a dying industry, and as it was sitting on a ton of money, the firm wanted to diversify into other industries. The right thing to do would have been to return the money to shareholders in the form of dividends, but instead the firm bought a fast food chain based in North Carolina. After the acquisition, the very proper executives and lawyers of the tobacco firm traveled south in their three-piece suits to meet their new employees, and came across a group of women in one of the restaurants. "What do you do?" an executive asked them. "We're FFMs," was the response. "What's that?" asked a lawyer. "We're finger-f___ mammas." The merger wasn't a success.

People like Michael Milken realized that the conglomerates were too large and too diversified. Executives had lost touch with their separate divisions, and the managers didn't know how to run them. Breaking up a conglomerate was expected to increase the value of the separate parts, and the evidence shows that it did. Busting up the corporate behemoths produced enormous wealth gains in our economy.[3]

If America is like a giant conglomerate, with the federal government trying to make rules for South Carolina and California and everything in between, we might be gaining less from economies of scale than we lose from being overlarge. We may need deconglomerization in the form of secession, and the people behind Calexit would be doing the political version of what Michael Milken did in the corporate world.

Next, let's look at how, simply as an exit option, secession might impose costs.

Underinvestment

Under the compact theory of federalism, a state could secede whenever it wanted, or at least whenever it asserted that the federal government was in breach of the Constitution. This possibility would come at a cost, however, since it would reduce the incentives for the country to invest in valuable joint projects.

That's what Lincoln had in mind when he lampooned the idea of secession by likening it to a "free love" marriage,[4] one which either party could exit at will. That would have seemed silly to most people in 1861, but it's what no-fault divorce has given us. Under no-fault, each marriage partner has the right to seek a divorce without alleging matrimonial fault, and in all but three states this right cannot be waived. This weakens the incentive to stay faithful to your spouse and increases the likelihood of divorce. Consequently, fewer married couples have children.[5] It's not that they don't want children. Instead, it's that the value of a child to parents depends on the expectation that the family bond will be permanent. Children are wanted more when a couple think they'll stay together, and wanted less when being a parent means a Happy Meal and a kids' movie every other weekend.

Likewise, if states had unfettered secession rights, they would be less willing to invest in long-term projects such as infrastructure for the country as a whole. Suppose, for example, that the federal government is presented with a plan for an interstate pipeline, whose benefits would greatly exceed its costs. The investment will require multiyear spending by the federal government, funded by taxpayers in all the states. But what if one state might secede before the project is fully paid for, and fail to contribute to it thereafter? Anticipating this possibility, the federal government might discount the project's benefits, and the opportunity might be abandoned.

Take it one step further, and imagine if our Constitution had a twenty-year sunset clause. Every twenty years the states would revert to full independence and the Constitution would be up for renegotiation. That's what Jefferson proposed in a famous letter he wrote to Madison: As the earth belongs in usufruct to the living, and as there's a new generation about every two decades, constitutions should expire at such intervals, he thought.[6] Consider what sunset clauses like that would have done to the federal government's incentives. What ships would have been built for the navy, when in a few years no one would know to which country they belonged, and whether to friend or foe?

Post-Constitutional Opportunism

When two parties enter into a long-term contract, they won't know in advance how it will turn out. It might be mutually profitable to continue fulfilling its terms for the entire course of the relationship, in which case the contract will be self-enforcing and we won't have to call in the lawyers. Alternatively, one party might find it advantageous to exit the contract and pay damages for breach. But there's a third possibility, where the contract continues to be mutually advantageous but the breakup costs would be disproportionately borne by the parties. Both sides would lose if the contract prematurely came to an end, but one party would be harmed far more than the other. The second party would then have a threat advantage were he to ask that the contract terms be renegotiated his way. "I know I agreed to buy the widgets for $100, but I'm thinking $80 makes more sense. Or we could just call the whole thing off."

That's called post-contractual opportunism. It's post-contractual because it happens after the formation of the contract and while it's still on foot, and it's opportunism because it's an attempt to use a threat advantage to extract better terms to which the party has no right.[7] When one state has secession rights, something very similar might happen, which might be called post-constitutional opportunism.

Suppose that secession would be costly for both the seceding state and the rest of the country, but that these costs are differentially borne and that the separation would be far less burdensome for the seceding state. It might then threaten to secede unless more of the federal government's revenues were directed its way. Many Canadians think that the Quebeckers acted in just this manner, until the rest of Canada tired of it and called their bluff.

Meanwhile a sterile game of threat and counterthreat had occupied Canada for forty years. With all the wasteful squabbling, it was like a painful marriage, not bad enough for everyone to call it quits but not very happy either. Ask a Canadian whether he likes the idea of secession rights, and he'll probably say no.

Transaction Costs

Sometimes secession is like ripping off a Band-Aid: just do it quickly. Czechoslovakia's breakup was like that, but I don't think it's what would happen in the United States. We'd have the precedent of the Civil War to get over, and the negotiations about the division of assets and debts would drag on for some time. Canada's lengthy debate over a possible Quebec secession gives us an idea of how it might unfold.

From 1964 to 1996, constitutional reform was usually at the top of the agenda of Canada's annual First Ministers Conference, involving the prime minister and the ten provincial premiers. For half of the last forty years, a separatist government has been in power in Quebec. The issue is off the table for the moment, in large part because Canadians are good and sick of it. But it has diverted attention from other things the government might have been doing, and that's a cost.

The same kind of cost arises in private law bargaining, and the Nobel laureate Ronald Coase gave it a name: transaction costs. These are the costs, in both the direct expenses of bargaining and the distraction from other opportunities, incurred when the parties negotiate to reach an agreement. The costs are greater when more parties must be joined in the agreement, because there will generally be a few malcontents and holdouts when the number of parties exceeds five or six. In Canada, the Meech Lake Accord of Brian Mulroney, the Tory prime minister, might finally have resolved the Quebec crisis, but it fell apart when a single Manitoba legislator objected that aboriginal groups had not been separately consulted. The accord needed all provinces on board, and the Manitoba legislature required unanimity on the question. So that was that. In the next general federal election, the governing Tory Party was virtually wiped out, so sick were the voters of the focus on constitutional matters.

Exit versus Voice

The grant of secession rights would deprive those who remain of the useful views of those who leave. That's an argument made by A. O. Hirschman in *Exit, Voice, and Loyalty*.[8] People who feel marginalized by a country have two options, said Hirschman. They can choose to exit, by emigrating, or they can voice their opinions and work from within to fix the problem. The voice option might be superior, but it might not be employed when it's easy to exit the country. Similarly, it might be better for a dissatisfied state to argue its case through democratic debate within the union, employing its voice and not its exit option. But there are two kinds of situations where the voice option isn't suitable.

First, the voice option does not commend itself when the seceding state is clearly in the wrong. In 1861, we didn't need to hear South Carolina voice its defense of slavery. The state's position on the issue made secession wrongful, and so the Union was right to deny exit rights.

Second, the voice option doesn't work when both sides shut their ears to reasoned debate about the issues that divide them. And that's where we are in 2020. Sixty-three million people voted for Donald Trump in 2016, nearly half of all voters. For much of the media and the academy, they are the enemy. Those who supported Brett Kavanaugh's nomination to the Supreme Court were "complicit in evil," according to Senator Cory Booker (D-NJ). You are either contributing to a wrong or you are fighting against it, he said. Trump is destroying democracy, and his voters need to be held accountable, echoed the *Washington Monthly*.[9] Hillary was right, said Jennifer Rubin. They really are deplorable, in the end. "Those who after all of that still back him either share his racist beliefs or have an incredibly high tolerance for racism."[10] After the mass murder in El Paso in August 2019, the vitriol was turned up a notch. Not merely is Trump a white nationalist, but so are all his supporters and we're not about to forgive and forget them. When that's how people feel, they're past talking to each other.

The Evidence

In this chapter we've seen the benefits of bigness and the costs of secession. For the United States, it is by no means clear that these benefits outweigh the blessings of smallness as seen in the previous chapters. Even on their own terms, the wealth advantages of bigness are muted. As for the costs of secession, they might be smaller than the benefits of a breakup when a country resembles an overlarge conglomerate, in which the costs of bigness exceed the advantages.

The evidence shown in Tables 9.1 and 9.2 in the Appendix suggests that bigness is not an economic advantage for a country. Table 9.1 reports on how a country's size (in population) is related to its wealth (logged GDP per capita), and finds that larger countries are less wealthy. The advantages of bigness, in terms of things like internal free trade, don't appear to outweigh the disadvantages. Table 9.2 reports on government spending in relation to GDP, and it doesn't show much by way of evidence that economies of scale bring an advantage to big countries.[11] Like a huge conglomerate whose managers are incompetent to oversee its varied divisions, an overlarge country wastes resources because its officials can't govern it efficiently.

Of the 148 countries examined in Tables 9.1 and 9.2, nearly all are smaller than the United States. In general, they're all too big if the goal is to maximize a country's per capita GDP. If smaller countries such as Czechoslovakia could benefit from a breakup, then wouldn't large countries like China, Russia and the United States benefit even more? We're too large and too centralized, like a 1970s conglomerate, and isn't that an argument for a political version of Michael Milken's breakup, deconglomerization mergers?

Other countries have been able to bargain their way past the barriers to secession. When our country is so overcentralized in governance but so divided politically, when the level of mistrust is so high, when partisan rancor blocks needed reforms, the costs of secession might be smaller than the costs of remaining united. Unless we could find another solution to our discontents.

PART III

~

LESSER CURES

The states ... have the right, and are in duty bound,
to interpose for arresting the progress of the evil.
—Virginia Resolutions of 1798

10

SECESSION LITE

If the United States is too big, if it's too centralized and the states have ceded too much of their power to the federal government, that may be an argument for secession. But there are other, less dramatic possibilities, and one of them is *secession lite*, where a state simply legislates over or ignores a valid federal rule. It's nothing new, and it happens in both blue and red states.

It began with the doctrine of *nullification*, in which states claimed the power to declare a federal statute void within their borders. If the Constitution was simply a compact among the states and the federal government, then a state might have the right to interpret the Constitution as it wished, and nullification might make sense. But the doctrine was rejected by the federal government and by most states even before the Civil War, and no longer survives.

Short of nullification, a state might do everything in its power to frustrate a federal law to which it objects. This lesser power, called *interposition*, was invented by James Madison in 1798, and since he so conspicuously failed to persuade the Framers to adopt his ideas at the Constitutional Convention, since all his cherished ideas in the Virginia Plan were ground into dust,[1] this was his principal contribution to the structure of American government as a constitutional draftsman. In the age of Trump, we're seeing a good deal of state interposition, and it's a nice question just how far a state can go in opposing a federal law before this turns into an unconstitutional attempt at nullification.

Nullification

In 1798, when revolutionary France made war on its neighbors and its navy attacked American shipping, John Adams signed into law the Alien and Sedition Acts. These allowed the president to imprison and deport noncitizens who were deemed dangerous, and criminalized "false, scandalous and malicious" statements that were critical of the federal government or the president.[2] Many Americans regarded these laws as a partisan, High Federalist attack on First Amendment civil liberties, and the popular unease with the laws helped elect Thomas Jefferson and his Democratic-Republican Party in 1800.

In office, Jefferson and his allies soon repealed three of the more illiberal statutes. Even before then, Jefferson had argued for the right of a state to nullify a federal law in the Kentucky Resolutions, which he wrote and which that state passed in 1798 and 1799. The resolutions declared that the Alien and Sedition Acts were unconstitutional, and that they were void and null within the state. On joining the Union by ratifying the Constitution, Kentucky had entered into a compact whose terms were the Constitution, and the federal government could not alter it unilaterally, or even assert the exclusive right to interpret it. The Constitution was like a contract in the state of nature, where there was no common judge, and where every party had "an equal right to judge for itself."

No other state joined Kentucky in support of a right of nullification, and with the repeal of the Alien and Sedition laws the Kentucky Resolutions became moot. The question whether a state could veto a federal law arose again, however, most notably in the nullification crisis of 1832. John C. Calhoun had argued that states could nullify federal laws even if they were otherwise constitutional, and South Carolina declared that federal tariff laws were null and void within that state. To back up this declaration, the state threatened secession if the federal government refused to respect the purported nullification. Indeed, if a state could nullify one federal law, it might nullify all of them, and in theory there is no difference between the doctrines of nullification and secession. But President Andrew Jackson forcefully stared down South Carolina, and when Congress relaxed its tariff duties in 1833 the dispute was tabled.

The question of a state's right to veto a federal law lingered in the constitutional shadows, and was not even wholly laid to rest by the Civil War. In the 1950s, several southern states embarked on a plan of "massive resistance" to court-ordered desegregation, and Arkansas amended its state constitution to maintain segregated schools. But this amendment was struck down by the Supreme Court in *Cooper v. Aaron*,[3] along with the theory that a state could veto federal law. The Court ruled that the Constitution's Supremacy Clause[4] made the Constitution the supreme law of the land, and that the desegregation decision in *Brown v. Board of Education*[5] was binding on the states. And this was finally the end of the nullification doctrine.

Interposition

If Jefferson was the captain of the Democratic-Republican Party, Madison was the second-in-command, the man who would succeed him as president in 1809. But the two were very different. As the ambassador to France on the eve of the French Revolution, Jefferson belonged to the radical-chic set that would later sign the death order for Louis XVI, and he returned to America in 1789 "in the fervor of natural rights, and zeal for reformation."[6] Madison was much more cautious and legalistic, a man whom a fellow delegate at the Philadelphia Convention described as "a Gentleman of great modesty, —with a remarkable sweet temper."[7]

Jefferson and Madison collaborated on their party's response to the Alien and Sedition Acts. But while Jefferson thought that a state could nullify a federal law it deemed unconstitutional, Madison was unwilling to go that far. Instead, the 1798 Virginia Resolutions, which he drafted, declared the state's "warm attachment" to the Union and "the most scrupulous fidelity" to the Constitution. Nothing was said of nullification, but when the federal government passed an unconstitutional act, said Madison, the states had the right and duty "to interpose for arresting the progress of the evil."

"Interpose" is a studiously vague term. Two years later, in a

20,000-word essay, Madison tried to clarify what he meant by it. As a matter of constitutional theory, he denied that the Supreme Court had the sole authority to interpret the Constitution, but as a matter of practice he spoke only of a state's right to communicate its objections with other states, petition Congress for redress, propose constitutional amendments and call for a constitutional convention. Madison was content to leave open what might be needed if all this failed, apart from referring to such "farther measures that might become necessary and proper." But during the nullification crisis of 1832, he sided with Jackson and concluded that states could not nullify a federal law.

The question raised by the doctrine of interposition is how far a state may go in objecting to a federal law, short of an unconstitutional attempt to nullify it. The extreme case would be a federal law so unpopular in a state that everyone within it would refuse to participate in its enforcement. Legislatures would do everything in their power to frustrate the act, and juries would refuse to convict.[8] That's interposition, and we saw it in the South before the Civil War. In such cases, there would be no way to enforce federal legislation short of sending in the troops, as James Buchanan realized.

If that's not on the horizon, there are still a good many federal laws that can't easily be enforced because of limits on federal resources or the possibility of jury nullification. Today, drug laws are a prominent example. The federal Controlled Substances Act outlaws the use of marijuana,[9] and punishment for offenders can be very steep. If they could, many states would nullify the federal law, at least for recreational or medical users. They can't, but California, Colorado and nine other states have legalized marijuana for personal use as far as state criminal law is concerned. This reflects the belief that the war on drugs has been a failure and has given too many people a criminal record. In California, for-profit private businesses are even permitted to sell the drug. As for the federal prohibition, no one taking a stroll down the boardwalk in Venice, California, would think that the drug is illegal. That's because the federal government has chosen not to send in the Drug Enforcement Agency to arrest anyone. The Obama administration announced that federal prosecution was not a priority, and even the Trump administration has given up trying to enforce the law. The federal government has limited resources to enforce all its laws, and if it tried to police California pot users, local juries might nullify the law by refusing to convict.

Until relatively recently, jury nullification in the South kept Ku Klux Klan murderers out of jail. But civil libertarians too have often championed the ability of juries to ignore laws they think unjust. Back in 1734, a jury refused to follow the judge's instructions and convict John Peter Zenger for libeling a royal governor in his *New York Weekly Journal*, and this has always been regarded as a victory for freedom of the press. American juries also refused to convict patriots of sedition before the Revolutionary War. In more recent times, jury nullification has been defended in cases where African American juries refused to convict black defendants for drug offenses.[10]

Jury nullification in California became an election issue in 2015 when Jose Ines Garcia Zarate, an illegal immigrant from Mexico, fired a gun that killed a young woman, Kate Steinle. At trial the jury acquitted him of murder since Steinle was struck on a ricochet, but it also acquitted him of involuntary manslaughter, which looked like jury nullification. Federal immigration laws are very unpopular in San Francisco, where Garcia Zarate was tried.

Garcia Zarate had been deported five times, and he always returned to California. He had seven prior felony convictions, including posses- sion of heroin and manufacturing narcotics. Before killing Steinle, he had been in a San Francisco jail, and U.S. Immigration and Customs Enforcement (ICE) had tried to deport him. It issued a detainer so they could apprehend him on his release from jail, but San Francisco is a "sanctuary city" that restricts cooperation with ICE to cases of violent felony charges. The city ignored the detainer and released Garcia Zarate onto the streets ten weeks before he killed Steinle.[11]

California is correct in asserting that, as a matter of constitutional law, its public officials cannot be compelled to assist federal authorities in the enforcement of federal laws. That's a principle that goes back to an 1842 decision in which Justice Joseph Story held that the federal government could not commandeer state officials to implement the Fugitive Slave Act and return slaves to their masters.[12] Nevertheless, California officials seem to go out of their way to stop the feds from enforcing federal immigration laws. For example, Oakland's mayor, Libby Schaaf (D), warned the city's illegals to lie low when she learned of an impending immigration raid. This prevented federal officials from making eight hundred arrests, according to the head of the immigration service. It's "no better than a gang lookout yelling 'Police!' when a police cruiser comes in the neighborhood," said an ICE official.[13]

In Portland, Oregon, the mayor went a step further when an ICE building was surrounded by protesters and its workers feared for their safety. The mayor supported the protesters, and the local police, following his orders, refused to take sides. The ICE workers were effectively imprisoned in their building until federal forces from the Department of Homeland Security arrived to rescue them. When it was over, Homeland Security installed a "no-climb" fence to protect the ICE workers, and the city complained that it was too high.

San Francisco's sanctuary ordinances prevent city employees from revealing when nonviolent felons will be discharged from state prisons, so as to keep them from being deported. In 2017 this policy was legislated statewide under California's sanctuary law. The U.S. attorney general, Jeff Sessions, likened the law to an act of secession, and he sued to set it aside. In response, Governor Jerry Brown tweeted that the federal government was "basically going to war" with his state: "At a time of unprecedented political turmoil, Jeff Sessions has come to California to further divide and polarize America. Jeff, these political stunts may be the norm in Washington, but they don't work here. SAD!!!"[14]

California has also gone as far as it can to prevent employers from discriminating against illegal aliens in hiring decisions. The federal government's E-Verify program permits businesses to access a federal database to determine whether an employee has the right to work in the United States. However, California prevents its municipalities from requiring employers to use the database. The state also bans employers from permitting federal immigration officials to enter their places of business or review employment records without a court order.[15] What would the response be, asked the attorney general, if a polluting state barred its businesses from allowing EPA officials to enter their factories?[16]

The interposition game has been played by both liberals and conservatives, depending on which party controls the White House. During the Obama administration it was conservatives who tried to work around federal laws, from the Affordable Care Act to federal gun laws. Proposed Missouri gun legislation in 2013 would have amounted to nullification. The bill adopted the compact theory of the Constitution that the Kentucky Resolutions had asserted, and declared that restrictive federal gun laws were null and void in Missouri. Moreover, the bill made it a criminal offense for federal officials to try to enforce federal gun laws.[17] But before the state police could arrest federal officers, the bill was vetoed by the governor and the attempt to override the veto failed by a single vote.[18]

Because there's an overlap between the powers of federal and state governments, American federalism is inevitably a little messy. Sometimes that's a good thing. The overlap permitted the federal government to prosecute the 1964 murders of three civil rights workers in Mississippi. The state wasn't going to bring charges, but the federal government did.

We want the federal government to step in when the state law is horribly lax. But what if the federal government's laws are thought too strict? That's what many Californians think about federal drug laws. As the country becomes more divided, the expansion of federal power invites more pushback from the states, resulting in the kind of turf wars that Eric Posner and Adrian Vermeule call "constitutional showdowns."[19]

At the extreme end, a showdown can shade into nullification and a constitutional crisis. But that isn't always a bad thing. When the feds and the states contest a law, voters and officials then need to determine which level of government has the right of the matter. Even a delay in enforcement can make interposition resemble nullification. A state that uses every means at its disposal to neuter a federal law might render it unenforceable within its jurisdiction, at least until the Supreme Court is able to rule on the matter, which might be years later. During the interim, a new president may have been elected, and the new administration might take the state's view of the question. But even if this doesn't happen, the dispute will have served to inform the Court of the intensity of opinion on both sides, which might result in a decision that is better informed about the bounds of federalism. The conflict may be valuable if it clarifies alternatives and suggests novel solutions.[20]

Madison's interposition doctrine lives on, and that isn't a bad thing. It's a healthy alternative to the constitutional impasse of nullification or secession.

11

HOME RULE

We've been taught that the idea of secession is long behind us. It's not, and there's much to be said for an American breakup. We're no longer apt to hang out with people across the partisan divide, or work with them or even live in the same neighborhood. As a people we're too darn mean, and as a country we're too damn big. We would get along better if we split apart. The constitutional hurdles are far lower than most people think, and there would be no Abraham Lincoln to stop us.

Yet is that what we'd want? We may be less than enamored of each other, but we might be unhappier living apart. With secession, we'd be giving up the pride we take in belonging to the greatest nation on earth, the power and the glory. That counts for something. So does what Lincoln called the mystic chords of a common memory, even in a forgetful country that is asked to scorn the heroes of its past, to paint over their pictures. Therefore, we might want to find some middle way short of secession that lets us sort ourselves out.

We've tried it before. At the Washington Peace Convention of 1861, we tried to bargain our way out of an American breakup. Before that, the British government had tried bargaining to prevent the thirteen colonies from breaking away from the mother country. The Carlisle Commission of 1778 attempted to hold things together and make peace on generous terms, offering Americans a right of self-determination short of outright independence. It's what later became known as home rule, and though it failed in 1778, it might still be a way out for the fractious, angry and divided Americans of 2020.

The Halfway House

News of General Burgoyne's defeat at Saratoga in 1777 hit London with a thunderclap. The British had thought that the Americans were backwoodsmen who took potshots from behind trees, but now an American army had stood up to the British Grenadiers and forced their surrender. And the war was expensive. It was time to think of ending it.

George III was opposed to any deal with the disloyal Americans, and pointed out that the British position remained strong. General Washington's army was encamped at Valley Forge, and the British held New York, Philadelphia and Charleston, as well as command of the sea. Nevertheless, many British Whigs sympathized with the Americans, and most MPs were ready to sue for peace.[1] Even the Tory prime minister, Lord North, had had enough, and confessed that he wished to resign. At Parliament's bidding, a peace commission was sent to America to negotiate an end to the war.

The commission was headed by the twenty-nine-year-old Earl of Carlisle, a choice that was roundly ridiculed. Horace Walpole described Carlisle as "a young man of pleasure and fashion, fond of dress and gaming, by which he had greatly hurt his fortune, [who] was totally unacquainted with business, and though not void of ambition, had but moderate parts, and less application."[2] An upper-class twit, in short. The commission's secretary was a renowned scholar, however, the fifty-four-year-old Adam Ferguson. And the peace terms offered were more than generous: Britain would withdraw all its troops, pardon everyone and grant America the right of self-government. Parliament would not lay taxes upon America or regulate American trade without American consent. All the grievances that the Americans had set forth in the Declaration of Independence either had been or would be remedied. The one thing not on the table was independence.

It was the most favorable proposal the Americans could expect from Britain, short of a complete surrender.[3] But when Ferguson tried to cross the lines to meet Washington, the general politely declined. The terms offered by the Carlisle Commission might have been persuasive to many Americans, but the Continental Congress made sure that the news wouldn't reach their ears. Finally the commission withdrew.

Having committed themselves to war, the Americans were unwilling to make peace. They also thought that accepting the British terms would betray their new French allies. But agreeing to the proffered terms would have saved thousands of lives and anticipated the manner in which Britain's other colonies became self-governing, beginning with Canada in 1849.

What the Canadians got was a halfway house to independence, and all that was needed to make it work was an instruction that the royal governor sign any bill the colonial legislature sent him. Thereafter, Canada showed how the Westminster style of parliamentary government could be exported to a country very different from England in its language, religion and geography. In time, the colony became fully independent, when Britain surrendered the power to direct its foreign policy. This became the model by which fifty British colonies, comprising two billion people, acceded over time to independence. And that is no small thing.

The Canadian model of partial self-government was called Home Rule when Gladstone proposed it in 1886 as a solution to the Irish troubles. While maintaining its allegiance to the Crown, John Bull's other island might be given the right to local self-government under the Irish parliament in Dublin.[4] After long debate and an active rebellion, Home Rule was finally adopted and proclaimed in force with the Government of Ireland Act in 1920.[5]

The act did nothing to end the IRA's guerilla war. The establishment of a Northern Ireland parliament for the six majoritarian Protestant counties failed to pacify the country, and the law was superseded by the 1921 Anglo-Irish Treaty, which created the Irish Free State. The treaty's first article stated that "Ireland shall have the same constitutional status in the Community of Nations known as the British Empire as the Dominion of Canada," which by then was an independent country. The treaty's "Canada clause" further provided that the relation of Great Britain to Ireland would be as that of Britain to Canada, "and the law, practice and constitutional usage" of Canada would govern Britain's relation to the Irish Free State.[6]

By 1921, what the Canadian model offered was full independence.

Applied to a Calexit, this would be the equivalent of secession from America. Home rule would be something less than full independence, and more like what for a brief interlude the 1920 Government of Ireland Act had provided. It amounted to self-rule within Ireland, but left foreign affairs with the imperial parliament at Westminster.

Might that be a model for today's United States, not as a way station on the path to secession, but as a better restatement of the powers of the federal and state governments? It would be an exit option of sorts, but a limited one, because the federal government would retain important powers. At one time, federalism did the trick, but that was before the federal government expanded inexorably and state responsibilities shrank in proportion. Today, federalism is not healing the country's divisions, so something else is needed, something more like home rule.

Economic Self-Rule

Our current version of federalism has given us rule from Washington by a government bound hand and foot to lobbyists, resulting in countless regulations and regulatory crimes, where needed reforms cannot be enacted and wasteful laws prove impossible to repeal. We may want a fresh start, of the kind David Hume had in mind, "either by a dissolution of some old government, or by the combination of men to form a new one, in some distant part of the world."[7]

Washington has become the seat of a sclerotic society of special interests, hobbling the rest of us with wealth-destroying rules.[8] Much of this is done at the administrative level, with the rules published in the Code of Federal Regulations. The CFR contained 35 million words in 1970. By 2016 it had grown to 105 million words.[9] Since no one can keep up with the flood of new regulations, and since many of them provide for criminal sanctions with no requirement of a guilty mind, a criminal defense attorney has observed that the ordinary American might easily commit "three felonies a day."[10]

We could benefit by pruning them back, but once the regulations are codified there isn't much we can do about them. Before a rule is adopted, the Administrative Procedure Act (APA) requires agencies to issue a notice and allow a period for public comment. If that was designed to slow things down, evidently it didn't work. But it has worked in reverse.

The same notice-and-comment procedure is required before a rule can be rescinded, and here it functions as a brake. The APA was supposed to protect us from a regulatory nightmare, but it's had the opposite effect, preventing us from eliminating excessive regulations.

Conservative scholars would like the courts to tackle the problem, by subjecting the regulations to greater judicial scrutiny.[11] But lawyers and judges aren't trained in the scientific skills that regulators are called on to exercise. What courts offer is technical, procedural review, and not the kind of scientific and economic scrutiny that might tell us whether the rule is well designed and efficient. There's an administrative state in every First World country, and in each of them the courts necessarily defer to the regulators.

If the regulatory morass is worse in America than in many other First World countries, there's a reason for this. We're too damn big. The greater the distance between the government and the people, the easier it is for the special interests, the K Street lobbyists and the crony capitalists, to capture the apparatus of government and its regulations. It's the minoritarian misbehavior we saw in Chapter 6, with the government wastefully shifting wealth from dispersed losers in the heartland to concentrated winners in Washington by means of onerous rules. Since we see more of it in large countries, the administrative burden on Europeans became much greater when the European Union began writing the rules rather than the national governments, and that's why Brexit would mean regulatory relief for Britons.

Relief for us won't come from Washington, but it might come from a constitutional convention, with a new deal in which a state is accorded home rule within the Union. The federal government would likely retain full authority over foreign affairs, so that one part of the country could not become allied to an enemy of the other part. Madison was right to be concerned about that possibility at the Philadelphia Convention, and the powers granted to Canada and Ireland under Home Rule excluded foreign affairs. The 1920 Government of Ireland Act would also have preserved free trade between Ireland and the rest of Britain, and an American home rule could similarly prohibit the barriers to internal American trade that prevailed before the adoption of the Constitution. Along with the free movement of goods and services, we'd also want mobility rights and the free movement of American citizens. Even with home rule, Americans shouldn't need a passport to visit another American state. But a great deal of power would still devolve on a state that opts for home rule, particularly in matters of financial and economic regulation.

Not everyone wants the same degree of regulation. Given home rule, South Carolina would likely rescind many of the job-killing federal regulations. California, on the other hand, might ramp up with more regulations. And then we might each sort ourselves out by our decisions where to live.

It's called "Tiebout sorting," after Charles Tiebout.[12] Suppose that different states offered different sets of public goods in a federal state with no legal barriers to mobility.[13] Some high-tax states would have great roads, and some low-tax states would have terrible ones. At the margin, that will affect peoples' decisions where to live. Some will want good roads and short commute times and be willing to pay for them, and some will be willing to put up with the traffic on Chicago's Kennedy Expressway in from O'Hare. Now, suppose that moving between states were costless. What we'd expect to result is a perfect match of people and governments, of personal preferences and public policies.

Of course, moving isn't costless. U-Haul does charge for its services. But when so many of us move around already, that's less of a barrier than one might think, and the cost isn't so great in comparison with the benefit of settling in a state that suits you better. Apart from the financial costs, there's of course an emotional cost to leaving friends and family behind. But for many of us—those who have moved—this cost is outweighed by the costs of staying put.

Forty percent of Americans live in a state other than the one in which they were born. In California, it's over 50 percent.[14] Three-quarters of the people in Nevada were born somewhere else. For many Americans, the question is not whether but whither to move. Sometimes the choice is made by the employer, and we follow him to the new job. But the employer will also decide where to settle his business according to his preferences and the likely preferences of his employees.

In trying to satisfy voter preferences, local legislatures will know more than the federal government. That's what Montesquieu and Rousseau thought, and the Supreme Court agreed: "A decentralized government...will be more sensitive to the diverse needs of a heterogenous society."[15] When it comes to deciding what Virginia needs in the way of roads, for example, Virginia drivers and legislators will know best.

Once one abandons the assumption that the optimal set of rules for all can be determined through abstract speculation by scientific planners for a central authority, it becomes important to look for real-world evidence about what works. The best way to find it is to observe the locational choices made by citizens who vote with their feet, choosing one set of rules over others. When rules are nationalized, we lose this evidence, but home rule would help restore it.

When firms make their decisions about where to incorporate, they are effectively voting for a set of rules. After New Jersey tightened its incorporation rules under Governor Woodrow Wilson, companies that had incorporated in that state reincorporated in Delaware. Thereafter Delaware became the state of choice in which to incorporate for public corporations. It won the race because it had the most efficient set of rules.[16] When people decide where to move internationally, they likewise choose a better set of rules to live under. People flee corrupt countries and move to honest ones.[17] And within the United States, people flee the more corrupt states such as Louisiana and Mississippi and move to honest ones such as Oregon and Utah. That's the message in Figure 11.1, which reports on net migration (immigration to a state less emigration from it). The regression line slants upward from the corrupt states in the lower right, which people are leaving, to the more honest ones in the upper left, to which people are moving. Honest states are richer than corrupt ones, as we saw in Figure 6.1, and this makes them more desirable places to live.

Home rule would result in more competition between states to provide honest governance and the most efficient set of rules. But the competition could also become a "race to the bottom" in some ways. If states compete for migrants through their welfare payouts, they might have an incentive to reduce them in order to attract the employed and healthy, and discourage everyone else. States might then compete to see who can cut welfare the most.[18]

Home rule would also amount to an opt-out of national equalization programs aimed at ensuring that Americans in the poorest states are properly cared for. There are big wealth differences among the states, from New York at the top end, with a per capita GDP

FIGURE 11.1 PEOPLE MIGRATE FROM CORRUPT TO HONEST STATES

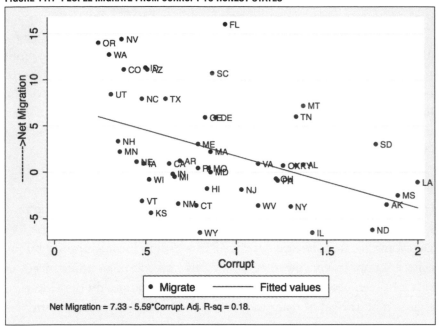

Net Migration = 7.33 - 5.59*Corrupt. Adj. R-sq = 0.18.

Sources: *Governing* Magazine, Net State Migration 2015–16 per 1,000 people; Dick Simpson et al., "Chicago and Illinois, Leading the Pack in Corruption," Anti-Corruption Report no. 5, February 15, 2012 (updated April 18, 2012), Table 7, Federal Public Corruption Convictions by All States and the District of Columbia per Capita 1976–2010, Convictions per 10,000.

of $75,000, to Mississippi at the bottom, with a per capita GDP of $36,000. Consequently there are huge differences in the welfare benefits offered by each state. To make things fairer, the federal government has its own welfare programs, which transfer wealth from "have" to "have-not" states. These include the more obvious welfare programs such as Medicare and Medicaid, as well as covertly redistributional programs such as Social Security. If home rule offered complete economic self-rule, a state could exit from federal equalization programs. That would give "have" states a greater reason than "have-not" states to embrace home rule. Since the "have" states are mostly liberal, they'd be torn between their oft-voiced concern about economic inequalities and their contempt for the Trump supporters in "have-not" states such as West Virginia and Alabama. For the Calexit people, that's no contest. They would be dumping the deplorables, and would have an economic incentive to do so.

Civil Rights

If you thought that welching on federal equalization payments might be controversial, how about opting out of the Bill of Rights? After all, it wasn't deemed to bind the states until well into the twentieth century. Before then, a state that wanted a bill of rights would have had to adopt its own, and many states did so. In the last hundred years, however, the courts have held that many of the rights in the Bill of Rights are "incorporated" and apply to the states. Beyond that, an expanding set of civil rights have been found to be lurking in the penumbra of the Fourteenth Amendment, concerning abortion and same-sex marriage, things that were highly contentious before the Supreme Court removed them from the political sphere. These rulings also restrict the states, and annoy conservatives. In other cases, however, the Court has angered liberals, in its decisions regarding gun rights and campaign finance.

Had these issues remained in the political domain, they would be subjected to the push and pull of public debate, and different states might go their own way. Instead, the Court's jurisprudence gives us winner-takes-all decisions, in which a single policy is adopted nationally across a diverse population, with Massachusetts values imposed on South Carolina and vice versa. And that's going to rub a lot of people the wrong way. Why should a South Carolinian care if Massachusetts bans guns? And why should a Bay Stater care if South Carolina permits open carry? Why should either care what another state does with same-sex marriage? With the opt-out that home rule would offer a state, the stakes would be lowered and we would all get along a good deal better.

But not so fast, Kowalski. Would we ever want to depart from our commitment to human rights? Human rights scholarship has always moved in the direction of an ever more encompassing set of principles, through international conventions and United Nations treaties. The search has been for the one perfect, Platonic set of rights, which when it's discovered can be imposed good and hard on everyone. Should the deplorable object, that simply proves that he's in need of political reeducation.

That's how the human rights community thinks, but it's an increasingly unpopular view. At the level of constitution-making, the movement has been in the other direction, away from a set of universal, fixed rules and toward a more nuanced set of human rights. It's been a move from judge-made law to the realm of politics, from the American Bill of Rights to the Canadian Charter of Rights and Freedoms.[19]

When the Canadian Charter was adopted in 1982, over provincial resistance, a federal code of human rights was watered down in two ways. First, Charter rights were made subject "to such reasonable limits prescribed by law as can be demonstrably justified in a free and democratic society,"[20] a clause designed to leave room for politics and the legislature, and to exclude what were seen as the excesses of American judicial activism. Second, the Charter's "notwithstanding clause" permits a province to opt out of Charter rights, as Quebec has done to preserve its language laws from judicial second-guessing. In this way, the Canadian Charter more closely resembles Thomas Jefferson's nullification doctrine and John C. Calhoun's constitution than the modern American one.

If that seems retrograde and illiberal, then some rights might be shielded from home rule opt-outs. The precedent here is the 1920 Government of Ireland Act, where Section 5 prevented the South from establishing a religion.[21] In Canada, provinces are barred from opting out of some Charter rights. These include gender equality rights, mobility rights (the right to move and work anywhere in Canada), language rights and minority language education rights. Provinces can, however, opt out of the Charter's guarantee of basic democratic rights, of free religious exercise, free speech, free assembly and many of the other rights in the American Bill of Rights.

The Canadian example is fascinating for two reasons. First, it shows that a modern state can adopt the nullification doctrine of Jefferson's Kentucky Resolutions and still be thought one of the most admirably liberal countries in the world. Second, the Canadian experience suggests that a state might be reluctant to use an opt-out right to legislate over the Bill of Rights. The Canadian Supreme Court decision in *Vriend v. Alberta*[22] is instructive on this point. The Court held that a private religious college in Alberta was barred from firing a gay professor. The Alberta human rights code had not referred to sexual orientation, but the Court held, remarkably, that the omission breached the Charter. All this happened twenty years ago, well before the gay rights revolution took hold. Nevertheless, the prestige of the Court and the moral suasion of the Charter were such that the province's conservative government let the ruling stand, rather than employ the notwithstanding clause.

Would an American state do likewise, given opt-out rights? If so, an American notwithstanding clause wouldn't much change things. We wouldn't see any state establish a religion, for example. There might be some variation around the edges, but the broad principles of civil rights would likely remain unchallenged. In that case, taking questions out of the judicial realm and letting the voters decide would tend to unite us, not divide us. We'd be more likely to recognize that we're really one nation after all, as the sociologist Alan Wolfe claimed.[23]

Or perhaps not. Wolfe wrote twenty years ago and we're a much more divided country today. Different states might now go their own way in human rights. That might not be a bad thing, however. Diverse sets of rights would permit Americans to settle in jurisdictions whose policies match their own preferences. Gun lovers could settle in Virginia, opponents in Maryland, and people would sort themselves out by voting with their feet. States that indulge in a taste for discrimination would likely be punished on migration markets, and states with superior laws would be rewarded.

That was the insight behind Frederick Jackson Turner's "frontier thesis."[24] Turner described a process in which western states and territories, with fewer geographical advantages, competed for people through liberal laws and democratic institutions. When Wyoming became a U.S. territory in 1868 it had a shortage of women, and so the territorial legislature, as a way of attracting more, gave women the right to vote in 1869, which is why it eventually became known as the Equality State. Eastern states, faced with the loss of valuable residents, responded by adopting similar legal regimes. The process, said Turner, even reached back into the Old World, where laws were liberalized to reduce emigration. This was a race to the top, won by states that offered the most desirable set of laws. If you want to find out what these might be, then let people choose.

With home rule, many Americans would resettle in states whose laws suit them better. It would be a kind of political and cultural sorting, but not like the forcible "ethnic cleansing" we saw on the breakup of the former Yugoslavia. It wouldn't be violent, as when Serbia fought its Moslems, and it wouldn't be ethnically based. It also wouldn't really be new to the United States. Today, for the Californians who want to keep their plastic straws, U-Haul is going gangbusters in renting out trucks bound for Texas. Home rule would simply accelerate the self-sorting.

There is nevertheless one last objection to opt-outs on civil rights under home rule. What binds us together as a country isn't a unique language, as in Finland, or allegiance to a dynastic house, as in Great Britain. It's not a distinct culture, as in France. Instead, the focal point for nationalist and patriotic sentiments is the sense that America has a special mission to promote liberty, as guaranteed by the Bill of Rights. This is what the historian Pauline Maier called "American Scripture."[25] A notwithstanding clause in our Constitution might therefore weaken our sense of national unity.

But as we're talking about secession, that train would already have left the station. There wouldn't be any movement to leave the Union if people hadn't already lost their desire for unity. Home rule might strengthen the sense of unity, then, if the irritants that divide us were removed, leaving a thinner set of countrywide rights. And this could be a welcome alternative to secession.

12

EVERYTHING THAT RISES
MUST CONVERGE

Dreaming, I was only dreaming...
—Billie Holiday, "Gloomy Sunday"

So there you have it. The barriers to secession are weak, the case for a breakup is strong. But is it really about to happen? In recent polls, support for secession has never reached 50 percent in any state. The Calexit movement has yet to gain traction, with a poll in 2017 finding that 58 percent of Californians preferred to stay in the United States, against only 25 percent favoring secession.[1] The movement wasn't helped when one of its leaders announced that he wanted to move to Russia.

Today the expansion of the federal government looks oppressive to some, and that makes secession appealing. But the fed's size is a double-edged sword, for it also makes secession harder to realize. Before the Civil War, when the federal footprint was so much smaller, people like Henry Adams thought that "secession was likely to be easy where there was so little to secede from."[2] The Statistical Abstract of the United States reports that there were only 36,672 federal civilian jobs in the entire country in 1861, and the Post Office Department accounted for five-sixths of them.[3] For South Carolina, all of whose federal employees resigned and were promptly rehired by the state, secession wouldn't have appeared all that disruptive, apart from the little matter of Fort Sumter.

It's different today. There are just over two million federal employees, excluding the military, and 33,000 of them work in South Carolina. Another 30,000 South Carolinians serve in the military, and 10 percent of the people in the Magnolia State are veterans who qualify for VA benefits. Federal aid makes up a third of South Carolina's general fund revenues, much of this for Medicaid and other forms of social assistance.[4] Once that sinks in, support for secession is likely to diminish, just as it did when Quebec separatists realized that they wouldn't be getting their welfare checks from Ottawa if their province seceded. Quebec federalists who opposed secession made a slogan out of it: *le fédéralisme rentable*. Profitable federalism.

America's fed-bashers are a little schizophrenic and even hypocritical at times. We complain about all the things the federal government has taken on for itself, but when it fails at any of them we're furious. We blame the feds even if there's been failure elsewhere, as happened after Hurricane Katrina in 2006. If one person was at fault for the devastation and loss of life, it was Kathleen Blanco, Louisiana's bumbling governor, along with the mayor of New Orleans, Ray Nagin (who now resides in a federal prison for bribes taken before and after Katrina). But it was chiefly President Bush who took the fall, with Kanye West complaining that "George Bush doesn't care about black people." Whether or not such criticism is merited, the buck stops with the feds when something needs fixing.

So we expect a lot from our federal government, and a good many of us depend on it for our livelihood. Even many private sector jobs would be affected by secession, more so than in 1861. At that time, South Carolina's principal export was cotton, headed for the mills of Lancashire. Trade with the rest of the United States was much less important. Today the national economy is much more integrated, and if one state were to secede it would have to worry about job losses caused by trade barriers with the rest of the country and with foreign countries with which the United States has free-trade agreements.

It might be that bigness is badness, that we'd be better off split into two countries. But which state will take the first step, as South Carolina did in 1860? Which state will begin the process, knowing how this would divert the government from all the immediately helpful things it can do, such as building roads and fixing potholes? Which state will pour oil on the passions of the day, and inflame them further? Which state will court the risk of invasion, of civil war? Which state will bell the cat?

Which people are willing to sacrifice the glory of belonging to the most powerful country in the world? Small might be beautiful, but you're more likely to believe this if you live in a small country. Finland will defend its borders but has no wish to extend them. It's only larger countries that to seek to dominate their region, or the world, and having done so they find it very painful to retreat into smallness. Churchill said he did not become prime minister to preside over the dissolution of the British Empire, and he didn't. That task he passed on to his successors, who presided over Indian independence in 1947 and the Suez debacle in 1956.

After Britain gave up its empire, America became the world's policeman. In a widely praised address at the American Enterprise Institute in 2004, Charles Krauthammer explained what this entailed: "If someone invades your house, you call the cops. Who do you call if someone invades your country? You dial Washington. In the unipolar world, the closest thing to a centralized authority, to an enforcer of norms, is America—American power."

The American Enterprise Institute's annual banquet is called the "neocon prom," and Trump's election was thought to mark a repudiation of neoconservative interventionism abroad. His campaign slogan was "America First." At his inauguration he said, "From this day forward, a new vision will govern our land. From this moment on, it's going to be only America first." But there is an ambiguity in the phrase, for it might refer to two different and quite inconsistent goals, both of which Donald Trump championed.

On the one hand, America First means realism and a retreat from foreign policy adventurism. On the other hand, America First might mean that the United States should seek glory, that it should be the world's greatest country, the country with the greatest economy, the most vibrant culture, the best universities. And also with the strongest military, one that Trump has begun to rebuild. That's also what America First means. It's what Krauthammer talked about in 2004, and his audience thrilled to it. They gloried in it. So do most Americans. And would those who voted to Make America Great Again now vote to make it smaller, through secession, and to surrender the glory of our military preeminence?

So we're likely to remain united. Nevertheless, it would be foolish to dismiss the possibility of disunion. It's the direction in which we're headed, and the notion that it couldn't happen again is fanciful. That's why we need to ask what might be done to restore the bonds of affection that have been so frayed. Home rule is one answer, but more generally what is needed is moderation from both sides, left and right but especially the left, in their desire to enforce their ideas about the good upon the rest of us. For starters we need a greater tolerance for differences of opinion. Paradoxically that's going to require a realization that people are permitted to dislike one.

Conservatives don't need to be told that they're disliked. In case they were wondering, all they'd have to do is watch some television, especially the late-night comedy shows. We've come a long way from Johnny Carson, and conservatives have learned to live with it. But liberals keep scratching where it doesn't itch and go out of their way to find offense. When same-sex marriages were recognized by the Supreme Court, they turned on a dime to take up transgender rights with equal passion. In the progressives' permanent war, there's always one more river to cross. They are like the southerners at the 1861 Washington Peace Convention who wouldn't take yes for an answer.

We'd also be better off if the courts intruded less in our politics. Too often, we've removed policy issues from the refinement they would receive through political debates and contested elections. Instead, we've permitted an unelected legal elite to decide what's best for us. Like the subjects of a nineteenth-century colony, we're told that we aren't quite ready for self-government. It's no wonder if some Americans might want to revolt against their rulers.

Most of all, I am tired of the haters, especially those who put up "No Hate" signs in their front yard to annoy their neighbors. With more self-awareness, they'd recognize that they are simply projecting their enmities. And with a greater understanding of the world, the separatists among us would show more gratitude that they're living in the greatest of countries.

And so I reveal myself to be a unionist, albeit one who wants to see a smaller federal government and a devolution of power to state governments. I believe that tolerance is better than fanaticism, and that ideological hatreds are especially dangerous because they're so enjoyable. I am quite certain that heart-easing laughter is a good thing, and would like to see more of our differences resolved over cases of rye whisky. I prefer sympathy to moralizing, and think that Teilhard de Chardin was not altogether wrong when he wrote that everything that rises must converge.

APPENDIX

A STATISTICAL PRIMER

The tables in this Appendix report on multiple-regression equations that seek to explain how one variable (the dependent variable) depends on several other variables (the independent variables). In Table 5.4, for example, we know what the happiness ranking (the reported subjective well-being) for each country is. What we want to know, and what the equations will tell us, is (1) what the happiness ranking is as determined by the independent variables, and (2) how well the model's happiness ranking differs from the actual reported happiness ranking.

We also want to know, for each independent variable, how much it contributes to the model's happiness ranking, shorn of the influence of each other independent variable. Mathematically it's complicated, but computationally it's simple, thanks to statistical software programs for regression analysis.

In regression analysis, a dependent variable y is estimated from one or several explanatory variables, though a regression equation of the following form:

$$y - \alpha + \beta x$$

where α is a constant and β is a fixed number or coefficient, which is multiplied by an explanatory variable x. Where there is only one explanatory variable, we have what is known as simple regression; if there is more than one, we have multiple regression. In a multiple regression, one examines how the dependent variable is affected by each explanatory variable, shorn of the effects of the other explanatory variables.

In Table 5.4, each of the columns represents a separate ordinary least squares (OLS) equation that estimates SWB happiness levels from the variables listed in the table's rows. For each of these variables there are different values for each country, and in OLS regressions a coefficient is assigned to the variable that minimizes the squared value of the distance between that value and the estimate of happiness for each country.

In Table 5.4 the coefficient is the top number in each cell, and is multiplied by the actual value for each country to estimate the happiness ranking. The lower number in each cell in parentheses is the t-statistic that measures statistical significance. Generally, any coefficient with a t-statistic greater than plus or minus 2.00 is statistically significant.

The OLS estimation technique is a canonical method of closely fitting the coefficients with the data. How well it does this is measured by the R-squared values. For example, if the R^2 in column 8 is 0.67, that means that 0.33 or a third of the data is not explained by the model. There are obviously things going on that the formula doesn't catch. But it does report on what makes a country happy.

TABLE 5.3 DEFINITION OF VARIABLES

Happy	World Happiness Report 2015–17
Density	World Bank 2016
OECD-BRICS	Dummy variable, 1 if a member of the OECD or a BRICS country, 0 otherwise
Sub-Saharan Africa	Dummy variable, 1 if in sub-Saharan Africa, 0 otherwise
Latin America	Dummy variable, 1 if in Latin America, 0 otherwise
Diversity	A measure of ethnolinguistic diversity, from Alberto Alesina et al., "Fractionalization," *Journal of Economic Growth*, vol. 8 (2003): 155.
Income Inequality	World Bank Gini Rankings
Conflict	Council of Foreign Relations Global Critical Conflict Tracker
Military	Military budget/GDP, SIPRI
Unemployment	CIA World Factbook
Freedom	Freedom House, Freedom in the World 2018
GDP/Pop	CIA World Factbook
Government Spending	World Bank and OECD

TABLE 5.4 OLS REGRESSIONS FOR COUNTRY HAPPINESS RANKINGS 2015–17

	(1)	(2)	(3)	(4)	(5)	(6)	(7)	(8)
Population (natural log)	-.10 (-2.10)	-.10 (-2.01)	-.14 (-3.51)	-.15 (-3.42)	-.12 (-2.84)	-.12 (-3.02)	-.10 (-2.14)	-.09 (-1.97)
Population Density		.00008 (1.76)						-.0004 (-1.22)
OECD-BRICS			1.39 (9.07)	1.42 (8.50)	1.37 (9.01)	1.26 (8.32)	1.32 (8.41)	1.31 (8.12)
Sub-Saharan Africa			-1.00 (-7.19)	-1.09 (-6.64)	-.78 (-5.10)	-1.09 (-7.35)	-1.02 (-5.33)	-1.03 (-5.57)
Latin America			.74 (3.99)	.71 (4.44)	1.00 (4.66)	.64 (4.30)	.91 (4.26)	.89 (4.23)
Diversity				.37 (1.19)			.50 (1.71)	.42 (1.36)
Income Inequality					-.02 (-1.59)		-.02 (-2.03)	-.02 (-2.07)
Conflict						-.73 (-2.29)	-.98 (-2.48)	-1.01 (-2.44)
Constant	5.63 (36.11)	5.62 (33.57)	5.57 (45.55)	5.44 (27.71)	6.01 (17.64)	.5.63 (43.12)	5.98 (16.85)	6.06 (16.51)
No. of observations	154	150	153	148	141	153	138	138
Root MSE	1.12	1.12	.71	.71	.70	.69	.67	.67
R^2	.02	.02	.61	.61	.64	.64	.67	.67

Note. Entries are OLS linear regression coefficients, with t-statistics provided in parentheses, based on heteroskedastic-consistent (White-robust) standard errors.

TABLE 6.2 OLS REGRESSIONS FOR CORRUPTION: CPI 2017

	(1)	(2)	(3)	(4)	(5)	(6)	(7)	(8)
Population (natural log)	-3.07 (3.20)	-2.91 (-2.99)	-4.19 (-6.57)	-3.73 (-5.86)	-4.19 (-6.31)	-4.16 (-6.21)	-3.83 (-5.54)	-3.96 (-5.39)
Population Density		0.005 (9.05)						0.005 (0.68)
OECD-BRICS			28.47 (9.86)	26.31 (9.17)	28.89 (10.23)	26.80 (8.29)	26.30 (8.65)	26.44 (8.71)
Sub-Saharan Africa			-8.71 (-3.66)	-1047 (-4.29)	-7.41 (-2.74)	-5.71 (-1.90)	-6.64 (-2.01)	-6.65 (-2.01)
Latin America			-1.99 (0.53)	-3.98 (-1.06)	-1.36 (-0.31)	-1.75 (-0.47)	-2.28 (-0.52)	-2.14 (-0.48)
Conflict				-15.21 (-3.78)			-12.09 (-2.70)	-11.79 (-2.62)
Inequality					0.03 (0.15)		-0.01 (-0.08)	-0.009 (-0.05)
Diversity						-9.05 (-1.47)	-4.60 (-0.80)	-3.73 (-0.65)
Constant	51.42 (16.93)	49.90 (16.02)	49.60 (19.66)	50.56 (19.82)	47.72 (7.85)	53.45 (14.56)	51.78 (7.87)	50.94 (7.54)
No. of observations	148	146	148	148	138	145	135	135
Root MSE	19.42	18.89	13.54	13.13	12.53	13.50	12.32	12.35
R²	.05	.10	.55	.58	.59	.56	.61	.61

Note. Entries are OLS linear regression coefficients, with t-statistics provided in parentheses, based on heteroskedastic-consistent (White-robust) standard errors.

TABLE 7.2 OLS REGRESSIONS FOR MILITARY EXPENDITURES 2017

	(1)	(2)	(3)	(4)	(5)	(6)	(7)	(8)
Population (natural log)	.14 (2.00)	.14 (2.03)	.19 (2.49)	.24 (2.78)	.17 (2.36)	.18 (2.32)	.24 (2.75)	.26 (2.76)
Population Density		.00002 (0.13)						-.0002 (-1.07)
OECD-BRICS			-.70 (-2.48)	-1.03 (-2.10)	-.63 (-2.23)	-.67 (-2.28)	-1.07 (-2.12)	-1.27 (-.2.23)
Sub-Saharan Africa			-.61 (-2.04)	-.10 (-2.10)	-.71 (-2.45)	-.59 (-1.92)	-14 (0.39)	-.07 (-0.20)
Latin America			-.95 (-3.08)	-.87 (-2.96)	-.90 (-2.90)	-.93 (-2.91)	-.81 (-2.66)	-.89 (-2.75)
Conflict						.31 (0.39)	-.08 (-0.11)	-.13 (-.18)
Unemployment					-.0005 (-.08)		.004 (0.66)	.002 (0.42)
GDP (natural log)				.31 (1.25)			.41 (1.67)	.51 (1.87)
Constant	1.45 (7.41)	1.44 (7.46)	1.78 (7.25)	-1.34 (-.57)	1.77 (6.91)	1.78 (7.14)	-2.37 (-1.02)	-3.24 (-1.27)
No. of observations	141	139	141	138	136	141	133	132
Root MSE	1.39	1.41	1.35	1.34	1.31	1.36	1.28	1.28
R^2	0.02	0.2	.10	.12	.10	.10	.14	.16

Note. Entries are OLS linear regression coefficients, with t-statistics provided in parentheses, based on heteroskedastic-consistent (White-robust) standard errors.

TABLE 8.1 OLS REGRESSIONS FOR FREEDOM HOUSE RANKINGS

	(1)	(2)	(3)	(4)	(5)	(6)	(7)	(8)
Population (natural log)	-4.79 (-3.44)	-4.92 (-3.40)	-6.40 (-5.15)	-5.06 (-4.32)	-6.30 (-4.71)	-5.97 (-4.74)	-4.40 (-3.59)	-4.48 (-3.61)
Population Density		-0.0008 (-0.72)						-0.001 (-1.13)
OECD-BRICS			41.12 (10.75)	33.38 (8.11)	38.58 (9.24)	38.80 (9.84)	29.02 (6.34)	29.45 (6.29)
Sub-Saharan Africa			-3.75 (-0.79)	-3.95 (-0.74)	.63 (0.12)	-5.66 (-1.14)	-1.86 (-0.31)	-1.05 (-0.17)
Latin America			19.28 (3.84)	17.75 (3.16)	19.53 (3.84)	17.18 (3.35)	17.13 (2.99)	18.18 (3.16)
Presidential				-9.31 (-1.88)			-11.00 (-2.17)	-12.13 (-2.35)
Diversity					-12.37 (-1.43)		-10.33 (-1.27)	-9.41 (-1.16)
Conflict						-15.27 (-1.91)	-12.93 (-1.37)	-12.28 (-1.30)
Constant	70.12 (17.29)	70.97 (16.60)	63.05 (15.47)	70.00 (18.62)	68.25 (12.34)	64.24 (15.54)	75.43 (14.44)	75.27 (13.72)
No. of observations	152	148	152	138	147	152	136	135
Root MSE	28.60	28.39	22.18	20.81	22.11	21.95	20.79	20.54
R^2	.06	.06	.45	.48	45	.16	.49	.51

Note. Entries are OLS linear regression coefficients, with t-statistics provided in parentheses, based on heteroskedastic-consistent (White-robust) standard errors.

TABLE 9.1 OLS REGRESSIONS FOR LOGGED GDP/POP

	(1)	(2)	(3)	(4)	(5)	(6)	(7)	(8)
Population (natural log)	-.12 (-2.15)	-.12 (-2.13)	-.14 (-3.66)	-.10 (-2.17)	-.15 (-3.66)	-.13 (-3.35)	-.11 (-2.19)	-.12 (-2.34)
Population Density		.0003 (9.59)						-0.002 (-8.72)
OECD-BRICS			1.24 (9.00)	.91 (6.06)	1.21 (7.81)	1.16 (8.25)	.88 (5.35)	1.04 (6.58)
Sub-Saharan Africa			-1.48 (-8.46)	-1.47 (-8.36)	-1.47 (-6.82)	-1.55 (-8.41)	-1.52 (-7.03)	-1.48 (-6.93)
Latin America			-.07 (0.39)	-.27 (-1.80)	-.09 (-0.51)	-.14 (-0.81)	-.32 (-2.00)	-.21 (-1.34)
Freedom				.008 (2.47)			.006 (1.92)	.005 (1.56)
Diversity					-.08 (-0.22)		-.03 (-0.07)	.15 (.44)
Conflict						-.58 (-1.64)	-.41 (-1.12)	-.35 (-0.98)
Constant	9.68 (55.01)	9.62 (54.63)	9.80 (67.79)	9.35 (32.35)	9.88 (49.70)	9.85 (65.08)	9.52 (27.78)	9.40 (27.36)
No. of observations	146	143	146	145	142	146	141	140
Root MSE	1.20	1.17	.73	.72	.74	.72	.72	.69
R²	.02	.06	.64	.66	.64	.66	.66	.69

Note. Entries are OLS linear regression coefficients, with t-statistics provided in parentheses, based on heteroskedastic-consistent (White-robust) standard errors.

TABLE 9.2 OLS REGRESSIONS FOR GOVERNMENT SPENDING/GDP

	(1)	(2)	(3)	(4)	(5)	(6)	(7)	(8)
Population (natural log)	-.56 (-2.24)	-.58 (-2.38)	-.84 (-3.55)	-.31 (-0.84)	-.81 (-3.34)	-.45 (-1.55)	-.22 (-0.60)	-.12 (-0.34)
Population Density		-.001 (-5.72)						-.001 (-3.09)
OECD-BRICS			4.92 (5.45)	2.21 (1.26)	4.72 (4.14)	2.67 (1.98)	1.69 (0.96)	.61 (0.36)
Sub-Saharan Africa			2.05 (0.79)	2.62 (0.96)	2.49 (0.82)	2.96 (1.12)	3.16 (1.04)	3.26 (1.08)
Latin America			.70 (0.78)	-51 (-0.47)	.78 (0.84)	1.07 (1.11)	-.09 (-0.07)	-.07 (-0.05)
Freedom				.08 (1.90)			.06 (1.26)	.05 (0.91)
Diversity					-1.29 (-0.43)		-.76 (-0.25)	-1.39 (-0.46)
Corrupt						.09 (2.25)	.03 (0.63)	.08 (1.36)
Constant	17.69 (21.44)	17.99 (21.63)	16.40 (23.48)	11.20 (3.90)	16.86 (11.80)	11.95 (5.84)	10.52 (3.62)	10.04 (3.51)
No. of observations	118	118	118	118	116	117	115	115
Root MSE	7.83	7.81	7.65	7.54	7.75	7.64	7.70	7.66
R^2	.01	.03	.08	.12	.08	.10	.12	.14

Note. Entries are OLS linear regression coefficients, with t-statistics provided in parentheses, based on heteroskedastic-consistent (White-robust) standard errors.

ACKNOWLEDGMENTS

I give thanks to the many people who've helped me: to Michael Anton, Larry Arnn, Darren Beattie, Nick Capaldi, Angelo Codevilla, David DesRosiers, Hans Eicholz, Ivan Eland, Allen Guelzo, Doug Jeffrey, Robert Jeffrey, Sandy Levinson, Don Livingston, Dan McCarthy, Jim Piereson, Stephen Presser, Jason Sorens, Matthew Spaulding, Al Regnery and Bob Tyrrell.

I also thank George Mason's Scalia Law School for its generous support. Esther Koblenz and Peter Vay at the Scalia law library and Susan Birchler were extremely helpful.

My heartfelt thanks to everyone at Encounter Books, to the production team of Katherine Wong and Vanessa Silverio, and the marketing team of Sam Schneider and Lauren Miklos, to Carol Staswick for her quite extraordinary work as the book's editor, and especially to Roger Kimball.

This book would not have been possible without the encouragement and invaluable organizational and editorial assistance offered by my wife, Esther Goldberg, whose help I cannot adequately acknowledge.

F.H. Buckley
Alexandria, Virginia
August 9, 2019

NOTES

CHAPTER 1—ONE NATION, DIVISIBLE

1 Marina Frasca-Spada, review of *Philosophical Melancholy and Delirium: Hume's Pathology of Philosophy* by Donald W. Livingston, *Mind*, vol. 110, no. 439 (July 2001): 783.

2 There is a recent philosophical literature on secession. First off the mark was Allen E. Buchanan, *Secession: The Morality of Political Divorce from Fort Sumter to Lithuania and Quebec* (Boulder, Col.: Westview Press, 1991). See also *Secession and Self-Determination*, NOMOS XLV, ed. Stephen Macedo and Allen Buchanan (New York: New York University Press, 2003). The classic statements of the South's right to secede are: A Virginian (Abel Parker Upshur), *A Brief Enquiry into the True Nature and Character of Our Federal Government* (Petersburg: Edmund and Julian C. Ruffin, 1840); Albert Taylor Bledsoe, *Is Davis a Traitor; or Was Secession a Constitutional Right Previous to the War of 1861?* (Richmond, Va.: Hermitage Press, 1907).

3 Edmund Wilson, *Patriotic Gore: Studies in the Literature of the American Civil War* (New York: Norton, 1994); James C. Cobb, *Away Down South: A History of Southern Identity* (New York: Oxford University Press, 2005); James C. Cobb, *The South and America since World War II* (New York: Oxford University Press, 2011).

4 Florence King, *Southern Ladies and Gentlemen* (New York: St. Martin's, 1993).

5 Chuck Thompson, *Better Off Without 'Em: A Northern Manifesto for Southern Secession* (New York: Simon & Schuster, 2013).

6 Christopher A. Cooper and H. Gibbs Knotts, *The Resilience of Southern Identity* (Chapel Hill: University of North Carolina Press, 2017).

7 *Dred Scott v. Sandford*, 60 U.S. 393 (1857).

8 Woodrow Wilson, *A History of the American People*, in 10 vols. (New York: Harper & Bros., 1901), 8:196.

9 Michael Fellman, *The Making of Robert E. Lee* (New York: Random House, 2000), pp. 275–76.

10 Dwight D. Eisenhower, *Public Papers of the Presidents: Dwight D. Eisenhower, 1960–61* (Washington, D.C.: Office of the Federal Register, 1961), p. 602.

11 Edmund Wilson, *Patriotic Gore*, p. 335.

12 Pennsylvania Commission, *Fiftieth Anniversary of the Battle of Gettysburg* (Harrisburg, Pa., 1913).

13 *Shelby County v. Holder*, 570 U.S. 2 (2013) (striking down a portion of the 1965 Voting Rights Act that required federal approval before southern states could change their voting laws).

14 George F. Will, "Save Your Confederate Money, Boys," *Washington Post*, December 28, 1995.

15 Dan Piepenbring, "Chick-fil-A's Creepy Infiltration of New York City," *New Yorker*, April 13, 2018.

16 Deroy Murdock, "Desperate Democrats Dismiss Trump's Executive Order," *National Review*, June 22, 2018.

17 Reuben Brigety, "What Will You Choose? How long will America's highest officials continue to support Trump's monstrous behavior?" *Foreign Policy*, August 17, 2017.

18 See, e.g., Margaret Sullivan, "Quick to vilify Antifa, but slow to explain it," *Washington Post*, September 4, 2017; Carlos Lozada, "How Antifa justifies stifling speech, clobbering supremacists," *Washington Post*, September 3, 2017; Mark Bray, "What the 'alt-left' Antifa activists actually believe," *Washington Post*, August 20, 2017; Perry Stein, "What draws Americans to anarchy? It's more than just smashing windows," *Washington Post*, August 10, 2017. Stein reports one anarchist saying, "'It takes awhile to get used to the label [of anarchist] because it comes with a lot of baggage,' LeMaster said. 'People assume that anarchism is so extreme. But I associate it with wanting everyone's needs to be met.'"

19 Jim VanderHei, "America, the Radicalized," *Axios*, October 7, 2018.

20 Mike Lillis, "Hoyer: Trump committed 'treason' in Helsinki," *The Hill*, July 17, 2018.

21 Editorial, "Voters shouldn't reward Trump's assault on democracy," *Washington Post*, February 29, 2016.

22 Daniel Henninger, "'You Cannot Be Civil,'" *Wall Street Journal*, October 11, 2018.

23 Rasmussen Reports, "31% Think U.S. Civil War Likely Soon," June 27, 2018.

24 Paul Bedard, "Poll: 39 percent back secession, strongest among Democrats, blacks," *Washington Examiner*, August 12, 2018.

25 See also Pew Research Center, "The Partisan Divide on Political Values Grows Even Wider," October 5, 2017.

26 On how Lincoln thought the southerners were bluffing, see Allen Guelzo, *Abraham Lincoln: Redeemer President* (Grand Rapids: Eerdmans, 1999), pp. 252–53. Henry Ward Beecher opined, "Take my word for it—all the barking will be done before the election and there will be no biting afterwards." Shearer Davis Bowman, *At the Precipice: Americans North and South during the Secession Crisis* (Chapel Hill: University of North Carolina Press, 2014), p. 241. For his part, Carl Schurz was disposed to think of secession as a big joke. "There had been two overt attempts [at secession] already … when the South seceded from Congress, went out, took a drink, and then came back. The third attempt would be, he prophesied, when Old Abe should be elected. They would then again secede and this time would take two drinks but come back again." David

Potter, *Lincoln and His Party in the Secession Crisis* (New Haven: Yale University Press, 1942), p. 12.

27 On Virginia, see Votes for Secession by County, April 04, 1861, Virginia Secession Convention, University of Richmond, https://secession. richmond.edu/visualizations/vote-maps.html.

28 Amy Mitchell, Jeffrey Gottfried, Jocelyn Kiley and Katerina Matsa, "Political Polarization and Media Habits," Pew Research Journalism Project, October 21, 2014.

29 Editorial, "The Never Conservatives," *Wall Street Journal*, October 4, 2018.

30 E. J. Dionne, "Turn outrage into action," *Washington Post*, October 8, 2018.

31 David R. Mayhew, *Divided We Govern: Party Control, Lawmaking, and Investigations, 1946–2002* (New Haven: Yale University Press, 2005), p. 76.

CHAPTER 2—WHEN SECESSION IS POLITICALLY CORRECT

1 On the right of national autonomy, see Wayne Norman, "National Autonomy," in *Handbook in Practical Ethics*, ed. Hugh Lafollette (New York: Oxford University Press, 2003), p. 591.

2 Jon Elster, *The Cement of Society: A Survey of Social Order* (New York: Cambridge University Press, 1989).

3 Francis Fukuyama, *Trust: The Social Virtues and the Creation of Prosperity* (New York: Free Press, 1996).

4 Pew Research Center, "Public Trust in Government Remains Near Historic Lows as Partisan Attitudes Shift," May 3, 2017; Esteban Ortiz-Ospina and Max Roser, "Trust," Our World in Data (2017), https:// ourworldindata.org/trust.

5 Josh Morgan, "The Decline of Trust in the United States," *Medium*, May 20, 2014.

6 See Ran Hirschl, "Nullification: Three Comparative Notes," in *Nullification and Secession in Modern Constitutional Thought*, ed. Sanford Levinson (Lawrence: University Press of Kansas, 2016), p. 249.

7 The Second Continental Congress's "Declaration of the Causes and Necessity of Taking Up Arms," July 6, 1775, expressly described the impending conflict as a civil war, were it to result in an armed struggle.

CHAPTER 3—SECESSION: A HOW-TO GUIDE

1 Lloyd N. Cutler, "Using Morals, Not Money on Pretoria," *New York Times*, August 3, 1986.

2 Russia, Belarus, Ukraine, Georgia, Moldova, Latvia, Lithuania, Estonia, Armenia, Uzbekistan, Kazakhstan, Tajikistan, Kirgizia, Azerbaijan, Turkmenistan, Czech Republic, Slovakia, Bosnia & Herzegovina, Montenegro, Croatia, Macedonia, Slovenia, Serbia, Kosovo. On the rise of secessionist movements following the end of the Cold War, see Ryan D. Griffiths, *Age of Secession: The International and Domestic Determinants of State Birth* (New York: Cambridge University Press, 2016).

3 Cass Sunstein, "Constitutionalism and Secession," *University of Chicago Law Review*, vol. 58, no. 2 (1991): 633.

4 *The Records of the Federal Convention of 1787,* ed. Max Farrand, rev. ed. (New Haven: Yale University Press, 1937), I.54 (May 31). (Hereafter, "Farrand.")

5 Farrand I.165 (June 8).

6 Farrand II.466 (August 30). Two firm nationalists among the delegates, Charles Pinckney and Gouverneur Morris, would have given the federal government the right to declare that a state of domestic violence existed, without regard to what the state legislature or governor might think. What if the governor was at the head of a rebellion, asked Morris. But Elbridge Gerry opposed "letting loose the myrmidons of the U. States on a state without its own consent," and the Pinckney motion failed. Farrand II.317–18 (August 17).

7 Abraham Lincoln, "Speech to Germans at Cincinnati, Ohio," February 12, 1861, in *Lincoln: Speeches and Writings: 1859–1865* (Library of America, 1989), p. 203.

8 Editorial, *New York Herald,* February 5, 1861, in *Northern Editorials on Secession,* ed. Howard Cecil Perkins (New York: Appleton-Century, 1942), 1:349.

9 Horace Greeley, *New York Tribune,* December 17, 1860, in ibid., 1:201.

10 Walter M. Merrill, *Against Wind and Tide: A Biography of Wm. Lloyd Garrison* (Cambridge, Mass.: Harvard University Press, 1963), p. 268.

11 J. David Hacker, "Recounting the Dead," *New York Times,* September 20, 2011.

12 *Ex p. Merryman,* 17 F. Cas. 144 (C.C.D. Md. 1861). The power to suspend the writ is found in Art. I, § 9, cl. 2, and as it is found in Art. I's enumeration of legislative powers Taney ruled that only Congress could do so. Taney's courageous decision recalls *Wolfe Tone's Case,* 27 State Trials 624 (1798), where on a motion for a writ of habeas corpus by John Philpot Curran the judge ordered the military provost-marshal taken into custody.

13 Brian McGinty, *The Body of John Merryman: Abraham Lincoln and the Suspension of Habeas Corpus* (Cambridge, Mass.: Harvard University Press, 2011), pp. 151–53.

14 See William H. Rehnquist, *All the Laws but One: Civil Liberties in Wartime* (New York: Knopf, 1998), chap. 2; Brian McGinty, *Lincoln and the Court* (Cambridge, Mass.: Harvard University Press, 2008), chap. 3. Two years later Congress tried to solve the constitutional difficulty by authorizing the president to suspend the writ under certain circumstances. But Taney had also held that, even with a congressional blessing, Lincoln lacked the power to imprison Merryman and impose martial law while the regular courts were in session, and once the war was over the Supreme Court agreed in *Ex p. Milligan,* 71 U.S. 2 (1866).

15 Editorial, *Chicago Daily Times,* April 9, 1861, in *Northern Editorials on Secession,* 2:674.

16 Mark E. Neely, *Lincoln and the Triumph of the Nation: Constitutional Conflict in the American Civil War* (Chapel Hill: University of North Carolina Press, 2011), p. 109.

17 See "Declaration of the Immediate Causes Which Induce and Justify the Secession of South Carolina from the Federal Union," December

24, 1860, at The Avalon Project, Yale Law School, https://avalon.law.
yale.edu/19th_century/csa_scarsec.asp; and "A Declaration of the
Immediate Causes which Induce and Justify the Secession of the State
of Mississippi from the Federal Union," https://avalon.law.yale.edu/19th_
century/csa_missec.asp.

18 Carl Schmitt, *Dictatorship: From the Origin of the Modern Concept of
Sovereignty to Proletarian Class Struggle* (Cambridge: Polity, 2014),
p. 118. See also Harry V. Jaffa, *How to Think about the American
Revolution: A Bicentennial Celebration* (Durham, N.C.: Carolina
Academic Press, 1978), p. 26; Steven Johnston, *Lincoln: The Ambiguous
Icon* (Lanham, Md.: Rowman & Littlefield, 2018), chap. 1.

19 Carl Schmitt, *Political Theology* (Chicago: University of Chicago Press,
1985), p. 5.

20 Farrand I.202–3 (June 11). Even the Supreme Court agreed. While
holding that the union was indissoluble, the Court nevertheless said
that "there was no place for reconsideration or revocation, except
through revolution *or through consent of the States.*" *Texas v. White,* 70
U.S. 700, 726 (1868) (italics added).

21 John Locke, *Two Treatises on Government* II.13 (New York: Cambridge
University Press, 1991), pp. 366–67.

22 James Wilson, "On the Study of Law in the United States," in *Collected
Works of James Wilson* (Indianapolis: Liberty Fund, 2007), 1:443.

23 Whether calls can be aggregated in this way is far from clear. Russell
Caplan, *Constitutional Brinksmanship: Amending the Constitution
by National Convention* (New York: Oxford University Press, 1988);
Robert G. Natelson, "Counting to Two Thirds: How Close Are We to a
Convention for Proposing Amendments to the Constitution?" *Federalist
Society Review,* vol. 19 (May 9, 2018): 50–60.

24 See Charles L. Black, Jr., "Amending the Constitution: A Letter to
a Congressman," *Yale Law Journal,* vol. 82, no. 2 (December 1972):
198; Michael Stokes Paulsen, "A General Theory of Article V: The
Constitutional Lessons of the Twenty-Seventh Amendment," *Yale Law
Journal,* vol. 103, no. 3 (1993): 734.

25 Nick Dranias, "Amending the Constitution by Convention: Practical
Guidance for Citizens and Policymakers," Goldwater Institute,
November 14, 2014.

26 Quoted in Russell McClintock, *Lincoln and the Decision for War: The
Northern Response to Secession* (Chapel Hill: University of North
Carolina Press, 2008), p. 108.

27 L. E. Chittenden, *A Report of the Debates and Proceedings in the Secret
Sessions of the Conference Convention for Proposing Amendments to
the Constitution of the United States* (New York: D. Appleton, 1864),
Remarks of James Seddon, p. 94.

28 *Prize Cases,* 67 U.S. 635 (1863).

29 *Texas v. White,* 74 U.S. 400 (1869).

30 Farrand I.291 (June 18).

31 F.H. Buckley, *The Republic of Virtue: How We Tried to Ban Corruption,
Failed, and What We Can Do about It* (New York: Encounter Books,
2017), p. 48.

32 Farrand I.462 (June 29).

33 Farrand I.466 (June 29).

34 Farrand I.469 (June 29), Farrand I.484 (June 30). Wilson was perhaps the most respected legal scholar at the Philadelphia Convention, and at the subsequent Pennsylvania Ratifying Convention he again described the breakup of the country as a possible alternative to union under the Constitution. James Wilson, November 26, 1787, in *Collected Works of James Wilson* (Indianapolis: Liberty Fund, 2007), 1:186–87.

35 Farrand I.314–15 (June 19).

36 Pauline Maier, *Ratification: The People Debate the Constitution, 1787–88* (New York: Simon & Schuster, 2010), p. 306.

37 James Madison, June 14, 1788, in *The Debates in the Several State Conventions on the Adoption of the Federal Constitution (Elliot's Debates)*, 3:414–15.

38 William E. Buckley, *The Hartford Convention* (New Haven: Yale University Press, 1934), pp. 18–19; Richard Buel, Jr., *America at the Brink: How the Political Struggle Over the War of 1812 Almost Destroyed the Young Republic* (New York: Palgrave, 2005), chap. 8.

39 A. G. Guest and Judah P. Benjamin, *Benjamin's Sale of Goods*, 6th ed. (London: Sweet & Maxwell, 2002).

40 Jonathan W. White, "The Trial of Jefferson Davis and the Americanization of Treason Law," in *Constitutionalism in the Approach and Aftermath of the Civil War*, ed. Paul D. Moreno and Johnathan O'Neill (New York: Fordham University Press, 2013), pp. 113–32.

41 William Wirt Henry and Charles N. Blackford, *The Trial of Aaron Burr and the Trials and Trial of Jefferson Davis* (1900; Whitefish, Mont.: Kessinger Publishing, 2006), p. 85.

42 White, "The Trial of Jefferson Davis," pp. 131–32.

43 *Ex parte Milligan*, 71 U.S. (4 Wall) 2 (1866).

44 *Texas v. White*, 74 U.S. 400 (1869).

45 *Reference re Secession of Quebec* [1998] 2 SCR 217, 161 DLR (4th) 385. See Ran Hirschl, "Nullification: Three Comparative Notes," in *Nullification and Secession in Modern Constitutional Thought*, ed. Sanford Levinson (Lawrence: University Press of Kansas, 2016).

46 An American court, in a state that holds voter initiatives and referenda, would likely have struck down the Quebec referendum under the single-subject rule. If a court finds that an initiative contains more than a single subject, it will be disallowed because it fails to elicit clear voter preferences. Richard J. Ellis, *Democratic Delusions: The Initiative Process in America* (Lawrence: University Press of Kansas, 2002), pp. 141–43. Complicating the issue and befuddling voters was the very point of the manner in which the Quebec government had obscured the questions.

47 In 1861, the southern states did announce their willingness to discuss the division of assets and public debt responsibilities. Jefferson Davis sent representatives to Washington to discuss this, and they arrived on February 27, the day the Peace Convention adjourned. Both Buchanan and Lincoln declined to meet with them, however.

48 The 1983 Vienna Convention on Succession of States in Respect of State

Property, Archives and Debts would require a seceding state to assume an undefined "equitable" portion of the national debt, but it has been signed by only 22 countries and not by Canada or the United States. Daniel S. Blum, "The Apportionment of Public Debt and Assets during State Secession," *Case Western Reserve Journal of International Law*, vol. 29, no. 2 (1997): 263–98. Seceding states that emerge from colonial rule, as America did in 1776, would begin with a clean state, however.

CHAPTER 4—BIGNESS AND BADNESS

1 James Boswell, "An Account of my last Interview with David Hume, Esq.," in *Boswell in Extremes 1776–78*, ed. Charles Weis and F. A. Pottle (New York: McGraw Hill, 1970), p. 11.

2 David Hume, "The Life of David Hume, Esq., Written by Himself: My Own Life," in *The History of England from the Invasion of Julius Caesar to the Revolution in 1688*, Foreword by William B. Todd, in 6 vols. (Indianapolis: Liberty Fund, 1983), 1:15.

3 David Hume, "Of the independency of Parliament," in *Hume: Political Essays*, ed. Knud Haakonssen (New York: Cambridge University Press, 1994), p. 24.

4 David Hume, "Of the original contract," in *Hume: Political Essays*, pp. 186–201. Earlier still, in *The Treatise of Human Nature*, Hume had explained how social contract theories were circular, insofar as they rested duties of allegiance to the state on a contract without explaining how the institution of contract or of promising could exist in the first place. F.H. Buckley, *Just Exchange: A Theory of Contract* (London: Routledge, 2004).

5 David Hume, "Idea of a perfect commonwealth," in *Hume: Political Essays*, p. 232.

6 See Mancur Olson, *The Logic of Collective Action: Public Goods and the Theory of Groups*, 2nd ed. (Cambridge, Mass.: Harvard University Press, 1971).

7 Hume also noted that "a small commonwealth is the happiest government in the world within itself, because every thing lies under the eye of the rulers," in "Idea of a perfect commonwealth," p. 230. In addition, Hume supported the American colonists and their right of self-determination before the American Revolution. Donald W. Livingston, "Secession: A Specifically American Principle," *Mises Daily*, January 15, 2013.

8 The two authors happily corresponded with each other. Hume initiated this, with a letter suggesting corrections to Montesquieu's remarks on English law, to which the Frenchman warmly responded. *The Letters of David Hume* (New York: Oxford University Press, 1932), 1:133, 138n2, 176. See Ernest Campbell Mossner, *The Life of David Hume*, 2nd ed. (New York: Oxford University Press, 1980), p. 229. Hume also appears to have been instrumental in a 1750 English translation of *The Spirit of the Laws*. John Hill Burton, *Life and Correspondence of David Hume* (Edinburgh: William Tait, 1846), 1:304–5.

9 Montesquieu, *The Spirit of the Laws* VIII.16, in *Œuvres complètes* (Paris: Gallimard, 1952), p. 362.

10 Montesquieu, *Grandeur of the Romans and Their Decadence*, in *Œuvres complètes*, p. 118. Montesquieu's ideas about the primitive virtue of a poor but equal society are not easy to reconcile with his later thoughts on how *doux commerce* served to temper the ferocious morals of barbarians and produce a moral peaceful society. *The Spirit of the Laws* XX.1, in *Œuvres complètes*, p. 585.

11 Montesquieu, *Grandeur of the Romans and Their Decadence*, pp. 80–82.

12 Jean-Jacques Rousseau, *Considerations on the Government of Poland*, in *Rousseau: The Social Contract and other later political writings*, ed. Victor Gourevitch (New York; Cambridge University Press, 1997), p. 193.

13 Robert Zaretsky and John T. Scott, "Philosophy Leads to Sorrow: An Evening at the Theater with Jean-Jacques Rousseau and David Hume," *Southwest Review*, vol. 91, no. 1 (2006): 36.

14 David Hume to Mme la president de Meinières, July 25, 1766, in *The Letters of David Hume*, vol. 2 (New York: Oxford University Press, 1932). See Robert Zaretzky and John T. Scott, *The Philosophers' Quarrel: Rousseau, Hume, and the Limits of Human Understanding* (New Haven: Yale University Press, 2009).

15 James Boswell, *Boswell on the Grand Tour: Italy, Corsica, and France, 1765–1766*, ed. Frank Brady and Frederick A. Pottle (New York: McGraw Hill, 1955), p. 278.

16 Douglas Adair is credited as the person who first identified Hume as the source of Madison's thoughts on government. See Douglas Adair, "That Politics May Be Reduced to a Science: David Hume, James Madison, and the Tenth Federalist," in *Fame and the Founding Fathers: Essays by Douglas Adair*, ed. Trevor Colbourn (Indianapolis: Liberty Fund, 1998), p. 132.

17 James Madison, "Vices of the Political System of the United States," in *The Papers of James Madison*, ed. Robert A. Rutland et al. (Chicago: University of Chicago Press, 1962–), 9:348.

18 Farrand I.136 (June 6). Martin Diamond argued that this speech converted the other delegates to Madison's theory of extended republics. However, the theory was not mentioned elsewhere in the convention, and there is little evidence to support Diamond's claim. Martin Diamond, *The Founding of the Democratic Republic* (Boston: Wadsworth, 1981), p. 37.

19 Farrand I.136 (June 6).

20 Farrand III.77 (italics in original).

21 Rousseau, *Considerations on the Government of Poland,* p. 193.

22 On how Morris was responsible for the separation of powers in our Constitution, see F.H. Buckley, *The Once and Future King: The Rise of Crown Government in America* (New York: Encounter Books, 2014), chap. 2.

23 Thomas Babington Macaulay to Henry Stephens Randall, May 23, 1857, in *The Letters of Thomas Babington Macaulay*, ed. Thomas Pinney, vol. 6 (New York: Cambridge University Press, 1981), p. 96.

24 David R. Mayhew, *Divided We Govern: Party Control, Lawmaking, and Investigations, 1946–2002* (New Haven: Yale University Press, 2005), p. 76.

25 See F.H. Buckley, *The Once and Future King*, chaps. 8–9. If we've seen less of this with Trump, it's in part because some members of the third branch of government—the judges—are in open revolt against a president they appear to despise.

26 A majority of Americans think that, when compared with other First World countries, our Constitution is only average (28 percent) or below average (29 percent). Pew Charitable Center, "The Public, the Political System and American Democracy," April 26, 2018.

CHAPTER 5—BIGNESS AND HAPPINESS

1 John Stuart Mill, *Utilitarianism* (London: Parker, Son & Bourn, 1863), p. 14.

2 World Health Organization, *World Health Statistics 2016: Monitoring health for the SDGs*, Annex B: Tables of health statistics by country, WHO region and globally.

3 John F. Helliwell, Richard Layard and Jeffrey D. Sachs, *World Happiness Report 2018*.

4 See Will Wilkinson, "In Pursuit of Happiness Research: Is It Reliable? What Does It Imply for Policy?" *Cato Institute Policy Analysis* no. 590 (April 11, 2007).

5 William Pavot, "Further Validation of the Satisfaction with Life Scale: Evidence for the Convergence of Well-Being Measures," *Journal of Personality Assessment*, vol. 57, no. 1 (September 1991): 149–61; Jonathan Shedler, Martin Mayman and Melvin Manis, "The Illusion of Mental Health," *American Psychologist*, vol. 48, no. 1 (December 1993): 1117–31. See generally Robert H. Frank, "Does Absolute Income Matter," in *Economics and Happiness: Framing the Analysis*, ed. Luigino Bruni and Pier Luigi Porta (New York: Oxford University Press, 2005), pp. 65–66.

6 Ron Chernow, *Washington: A Life* (New York: Penguin, 2010), p. 540. On travel in the early Republic, see T. H. Breen, *George Washington's Journey: The President Forges a New Nation* (New York: Simon & Schuster, 2016), pp. 78–81.

7 See Pauline Maier, *Ratification: The People Debate the Constitution, 1787–1788* (New York: Simon & Schuster, 2010), p. 84.

CHAPTER 6—BIGNESS AND CORRUPTION

1 Transparency International, Corruption Perceptions Index 2010, Long Methodological Brief.

2 *Citizens United v. FEC*, 558 U.S. 310, 360 (2010).

3 *McCutcheon v. FEC*, 134 S. Ct. 1434 (2014).

4 Matea Gold and Anu Narayanswamy, "Bigger Role for Donors this Year," *Washington Post*, October 6, 2016.

5 *Buckley v. Valeo*, 424 U.S. 1 (1976).

6 Lee Drutman, *The Business of America Is Lobbying: How Corporations Became Politicized and Politics Became Corporate* (New York: Oxford University Press, 2015), pp. 93–94. See also Jeffrey Milyo, David Primo and Timothy Groseclose, "Corporate PAC Campaign Contributions in Perspective," *Business and Politics*, vol. 2, no. 1 (April 2000): 75–88.

7 The Competitive Enterprise Institute reports that federal regulations impose a cost of $1.9 trillion on the American economy, or nearly $15,000 per household. Clyde Wayne Crews, *Ten Thousand Commandments 2017: An Annual Snapshot of the Federal Regulatory State* (Washington, D.C.: CEI, 2017).

8 "Money and politics: Ask what your country can do for you," *Economist*, October 1, 2011. See also Hui Chen, David Parsley and Ya-Wen Yang, "Corporate Lobbying and Firm Performance," *Journal of Business Finance and Accounting*, vol. 42, no. 3–4 (April/May 2015): 444–81 (lobbying is positively related to accounting and market measures of financial performance).

9 Brian Kelleher Richter, Krislert Samphantharak and Jeffrey F. Timmons, "Lobbying and Taxes," *American Journal of Political Science*, vol. 53, no. 4 (October 2009): 893–909.

10 Frank Yu and Xiaoyun Yu, "Corporate Lobbying and Fraud Detection," *Journal of Financial and Quantitative Analysis*, vol. 46, no. 6 (December 2012): 1865–91.

11 Quoted in Lawrence Lessig, *Republic, Lost: How Money Corrupts Congress—And a Plan to Stop It* (New York: Twelve, 2011), p. 123.

12 F.H. Buckley, *The Republic of Virtue: How We Tried to Ban Corruption, Failed, and What We Can Do about It* (New York: Encounter Books, 2017), chap. 16.

13 Farrand I.422–23 (June 26).

14 Farrand II.414 (August 25).

15 Charles A. Beard, *An Economic Interpretation of the Constitution of the United States* (1913; New York: Macmillan, 1935). Modern historians tell us Beard fudged the facts. See Robert E. Brown, *Charles Beard and the Constitution* (Princeton, N.J.: Princeton University Press, 1956); Forrest McDonald, *We the People: The Economic Origins of the Constitution* (Chicago: University of Chicago Press, 1958), pp. 98–99. See also Alan Gibson, *Understanding the Founding: The Crucial Questions* (Lawrence: University Press of Kansas, 2010), chap. 1.

16 William Z. Ripley, *Main Street and Wall Street* (Boston: Little, Brown, 1927).

17 Joseph E. Stiglitz, *The Price of Inequality: How Today's Divided Society Endangers Our Future* (New York: W. W. Norton, 2012), p. 244. Politically connected banks received larger bailouts than financial institutions that spent less on lobbying or political contributions. Benjamin M. Blau, "Central Bank Intervention and the Role of Political Connections," Mercatus Center, George Mason University, October 2013.

18 Malcolm S. Salter, "Crony Capitalism American Style: What Are We Talking About Here?" Harvard Business School Working Paper 15-025 (October 22, 2014). See Timothy P. Carney, *The Big Ripoff: How Big Business and Big Government Steal Your Money* (Hoboken, N.J.: John Wiley, 2006).

19 Cheol Liu and John L. Mikesell, "The Impact of Public Officials' Corruption on the Size and Allocation of U.S. State Spending," *Public Administration Review*, vol. 74, no. 3 (May/June 2014): 346–59.

20 Howard Ball, *Murder in Mississippi:* United States v. Price *and the*

Struggle for Civil Rights (Lawrence: University Press of Kansas, 2004), p. 84.

21 *U.S. v. Price*, 383 U.S. 787 (1966).

22 Douglas O. Linder, "Bending Toward Justice: John Doar and the Mississippi Burning Trial," *Mississippi Law Journal,* vol. 72, no. 2 (Winter 2002)): 731–79.

23 Buckley, *The Republic of Virtue,* chap. 10.

24 *U.S. v. Blagojevich*, 794 F.3d 729 (7th Cir., 2015), cert. den. ___ U.S. ___ (2016).

25 J.G.A. Pocock, *Virtue, Commerce, and History: Essays on Political Thought and History, Chiefly in the Eighteenth Century* (New York: Cambridge University Press, 1985), pp. 87–88.

CHAPTER 7—BIGNESS AND THE MILITARY

1 Farrand I.19 (May 29).

2 Farrand I.316 (June 19).

3 Farrand I.466 (June 29).

4 World Bank, Military Expenditure (% of GDP).

5 Dwight D. Eisenhower, *Public Papers of the Presidents: Dwight D. Eisenhower, 1960–61* (Washington, D.C.: Office of the Federal Register, 1961), p. 1038.

6 Gillian Rich, "Defense Stocks Fall As Trump Makes This Concession at North Korea Summit," *Investors Business Daily*, June 12, 2018.

7 William D. Hartung, "How the Military-Industrial Complex Preys on the Troops," *Common Dreams*, October 10, 2017.

8 Clay Dillow, "Defense Contractors Outgun Other Industries in Corporate PAC Donations," *Fortune*, July 15, 2015.

9 Charles W. Ostrom and Brian Job, "The President and the Political Use of Force," *American Political Science Review*, vol. 80, no. 2 (June 1986): 541–66; Patrick James and John R. Oneal, "The Influence of Domestic and International Politics on the President's Use of Force," *Journal of Conflict Resolution*, vol. 35, no 2 (June 1991): 307–32; Gregory D. Hess and Athanasios Orphanides, "War Politics: An Economic Rational-Voter Framework," *American Economic Review*, vol. 85, no. 4 (September 1995): 828–46; William G. Howell and Jon C. Pevehouse, *While Dangers Gather: Congressional Checks on Presidential War Powers* (Princeton, N.J.: Princeton University Press, 2007), pp. 65–66, Tables 3.2 and 3.3; Jong Hee Park, "Structural Change in US Presidents' Use of Force," *American Journal of Political Science*, vol. 54, no. 3 (July 2010): 766–82.

10 F.H. Buckley, *The Once and Future King: The Rise of Crown Government in America* (New York: Encounter Books, 2014), p. 313, Table B.4.

11 The Australia-based Institute for Economics and Peace reports similar findings in its 2018 study of militarization by 163 countries, looking at military expenditures, nuclear weapons, military personnel and international arms shipments. Russia came in near the top at 162, sandwiched between Syria and North Korea, while the U.S. was ranked at 160, France at 157, the UK at 154 and India at 147. Institute for Economics and Peace, *Global Peace Index 2018: Measuring Peace in*

a Complex World, Sydney, June 2018, at http://visionofhumanity.org/
reports (accessed June 2018).

12 Stockholm International Peace Research Institute, *SIPRI Yearbook 2007:
Armaments, Disarmament and International Security* (New York: Oxford
University Press, 2017), p. 353.

13 Editorial, "The Other China Challenge," *Wall Street Journal*, June 4,
2018.

14 Edith Sitwell, *English Eccentrics* (London: Folio, 1994), p. 141.

15 Friedrich Nietzsche, *Thus Spoke Zarathustra* II. 22, "On Self-
Overcoming," in *The Portable Nietzsche*, ed. and trans. Walter Kaufmann
(New York: Penguin, 1954), pp. 226–27.

16 Hans J. Morgenthau, *Politics among Nations: The Struggle for Power and
Peace*, 2nd ed. (New York: Alfred A. Knopf, 1954), p. 25.

17 Melanie Mason, "Single-payer healthcare could cost $400 billion to
implement in California," *Los Angeles Times*, May 22, 2017.

CHAPTER 8—BIGNESS AND FREEDOM

1 Francis Fukuyama, *The End of History and the Last Man* (New York:
Avon, 1992), p. 204.

2 World Bank, State of the Poor, April 17, 2013.

3 George Orwell, "The Freedom of the Press," unused preface to *Animal
Farm* published in the *Times Literary Supplement*, September 15, 1972.

4 Montesquieu, *The Spirit of the Laws*, Part 2, Bk. 11.6, in *Œuvres
complètes* (Paris: Gallimard, 1952), p. 397.

5 Others are the Polity IV measure of constitutional democracy, Tatu
Vanhalen's assessment of participatory democracy, and the measure of
contested democracy provided by Adam Przeworski and his colleagues.
They all come down to about the same thing. See Pippa Norris, *Driving
Democracy: Do Power-Sharing Institutions Work?* (New York: Cambridge
University Press, 2008), pp. 56, 61–71, 152–53.

6 On the small is beautiful hypothesis generally, see Wouter P. Veenendaal
and Jack Corbett, "Why Small States Offer Important Answers to Large
Questions," *Comparative Political Studies*, vol. 48, no. 4 (2015): 527–49.

7 Aristotle, *Politics* VII § 4 ("if the citizens of a state are to judge and to
distribute offices according to merit, then they must know each other's
characters").

8 William Easterly and Ross Levine, "Africa's Growth Tragedy: Policies
and Ethnic Divisions," *Quarterly Journal of Economics*, vol. 112, no. 4
(November 1997): 1203–50; Rafael La Porta, Florencio Lopez-de-Silanes,
Andrei Shleifer and Robert Vishny, "The Quality of Government,"
Journal of Law and Economics, vol. 15, no. 1 (April 1999): 222–79.

9 Farrand II.644 (September 17).

10 Jean-Jacques Rousseau, *Social Contract* III.2, in *Rousseau: The Social
Contract and other later political writings*, ed. Victor Gourevitch (New
York: Cambridge University Press, 1997). Dwight Lee makes a similar
argument about bigness. A state large enough to exploit all of the
advantages of bigness, in terms of economies of scale, will be so big
that voters will be unable to police the special interests that deflect
elected officials from pursuing the public good. Dwight R. Lee, "The

Impossibility of a Desirable Minimal State," *Public Choice*, vol. 61, no. 3 (June 1989): 277–84.

11 Alberto Alesina, "The Size of Countries: Does It Matter?" *Journal of the European Economic Association*, vol. 1, nos. 2–3 (May 2003): 306.

CHAPTER 9—BIGNESS AND WEALTH

1 Farrand III.30.

2 Claudia Goldin and Lawrence F. Katz, *The Race between Education and Technology* (Cambridge, Mass.: Harvard University Press, 2008).

3 F. M. Scherer, "Corporate Takeovers: The Efficiency Arguments," *Journal of Economic Perspectives*, vol. 2, no. 1 (Winter 1988): 76–77.

4 Abraham Lincoln, "Speech to Germans at Cincinnati, Ohio," February 12, 1861, in *Lincoln: Speeches and Writings 1859–1865* (Library of America, 1989), pp. 203–4.

5 Margaret F. Brinig and F.H. Buckley, "No-Fault Laws and At-Fault People," *International Review of Law and Economics*, vol. 18, no. 3 (September 1998): 325–40.

6 Thomas Jefferson to James Madison, September 6, 1789, in *The Papers of Thomas Jefferson*, ed. Julian P. Boyd, vol. 15 (Princeton, N.J.: Princeton University Press, 1958), pp. 384–91.

7 Timothy J. Muris, "Opportunistic Behavior and the Law of Contract," *Minnesota Law Review*, vol. 65, no. 4 (1980–81): 521–90.

8 A. O. Hirschman, *Exit, Voice, and Loyalty: Responses to Decline in Firms, Organizations, and States* (Cambridge, Mass.: Harvard University Press, 1970).

9 Nancy LeTourneau, "Why I Hold Trump Voters Accountable for the Mess We're In," *Washington Monthly*, May 24, 2018.

10 Jennifer Rubin, "If you still support Donald Trump," *Washington Post*, August 17, 2017.

11 These results are consistent with Pippa Norris's findings that a logged population variable was not significantly associated with measures of economic growth. Pippa Norris, *Making Democratic Governance Work: How Regimes Shape Prosperity, Welfare and Peace* (New York: Cambridge University Press, 2012), pp. 111–12, Table 5.1. Similarly, while Alberto Alesina and Enrico Spolaore found that greater size was associated with economies of scale for general public consumption (including transfers and payments), but not public investment and military spending. Alberto Alesina and Enrico Spolaore, *The Size of Nations* (Cambridge, Mass.: MIT Press, 2003), p. 160, Table 10.4. It's only in the latter two cases, however, that we would expect to find economies of scale.

CHAPTER 10—SECESSION LITE

1 F.H. Buckley, *The Once and Future King: The Rise of Crown Government in America* (New York: Encounter Books, 2014), chap. 2.

2 Sedition Act, of 1798, ch. 74, 1 Stat. 596.

3 *Cooper v. Aaron*, 358 U.S. 1 (1958).

4 U.S. Const. art. VI, cl. 2 ("This Constitution, and the Laws of the United States which shall be made in Pursuance thereof; and all Treaties made,

or which shall be made, under the Authority of the United States, shall be the supreme Law of the Land").

5 *Brown v. Board of Education*, 347 U.S. 483 (1954).

6 Thomas Jefferson, *Writings* (Library of America, 1984), p. 665.

7 William Pierce, "Character Sketches of Delegates to the Federal Convention," Farrand III.95.

8 Such a law was the ban on abortion in the Canadian Criminal Code. When the Crown Attorney failed to secure a conviction against an admitted abortionist, Dr. Henry Morgenthaler, it appealed the verdict twice (there being no double jeopardy barrier in Canada). But on three occasions the jury refused to convict, and this effectively rendered the law inoperative.

9 Controlled Substances Act, 21 U.S.C. § 811.

10 Paul Butler, "Jurors need to take the law into their own hands," *Washington Post*, April 5, 2016; Paul Butler, "Racially-Based Jury Nullification: Black Power in the Criminal Justice System," *Yale Law Journal*, vol. 105, no. 3 (1995): 677–725.

11 Lee Romney, Cindy Chang and Joel Rubin, "Fatal shooting of S.F. woman reveals disconnect between ICE, local police; 5-time deportee charged," *Los Angeles Times*, July 5, 2015.

12 *Prigg v. Pennsylvania*, 41 U.S. 439 (1842). See also *New York v. United States*, 488 U.S. 1041 (1992).

13 Thomas Fuller, "Immigration Agency Rails against Oakland Mayor's Warning of Raids," *New York Times*, February 28, 2018.

14 Roque Planas and Elise Foley, "Trump Administration Is 'Going to War' with California, Governor Says," *HuffPost*, March 7, 2018; Katie Benner and Jennifer Medina, "Trump Administration Sues California over Immigration Laws," *New York Times*, March 6, 2018.

15 California Code § 7285.1 (2017).

16 E-Verify is mostly a voluntary program, to which private businesses may opt in if they wish. To that extent, a California law that bans private employers from assisting ICE in checking employment records is not in direct conflict with federal law. However, most federal contractors are required to enroll in E-Verify, and were California to prosecute them for granting access to ICE, that would appear to cross the line between a possibly permissible interposition and impermissible nullification.

17 H.B. 436, § 6, 97th Leg., 1st Reg. Sess. (Mo. 2013).

18 Leslie Bentz and George Howell, "Missouri lawmakers fail to override governor's gun bill veto," CNN, September 12, 2013. See further James H. Read and Neal Allen, "Living, Dead, and Undead: Nullification Past and Present," in *Nullification and Secession in Modern Constitutional Thought*, ed. Sanford Levinson (Lawrence: University Press of Kansas, 2016), p. 91.

19 Eric A. Posner and Adrian Vermeule, "Constitutional Showdowns," *University of Pennsylvania Law Review*, vol. 156 (April 2008): 991–1048 (describing conflicts among the branches in the federal government).

20 See Vincent Ostrom, *The Meaning of American Federalism: Constituting a Self-Governing Society* (San Francisco: Institute for Contemporary Studies, 1999), p. 272 (through constitutional challenges, we might

"elucidate information, clarify alternatives, stimulate innovation, and extend the frontiers of inquiry").

CHAPTER 11—HOME RULE

1 Solomon Lutnick, "The American Victory at Saratoga: A View from the British Press," *New York History*, vol. 44, no. 2 (April 1963): 103–27.

2 Horace Walpole, *The Last Journals of Horace Walpole during the reign of George III, from 1771–1783*, ed. A. F. Steuart (London: John Lane, 1910), 2:122.

3 Robert G. Parkinson, *The Common Cause: Creating Race and Nation in the American Revolution* (Chapel Hill: University of North Carolina Press, 2016), pp. 61–76. Earlier, Loyalist Joseph Galloway had proposed a form of home rule in 1774 as an alternative to outright independence, and this was rejected by only one vote, six to five. Moses Coit Tyler, *The Literary History of the American Revolution 1763–1783* (New York: Ungar, 1957), 1:372.

4 *Hansard Parliamentary Debates*, 3d ser., vol 305 (10 May 1886, W. E. Gladstone), cols. 574–603. See David Fitzpatrick, "Ireland and the Empire" in *The Oxford History of the British Empire*, vol. 3, *The Nineteenth Century*, ed. Andrew Porter and Alaine Low (New York: Oxford University Press, 2001), p. 506.

5 Government of Ireland Act, 1920, 10 & 11 Geo. 5, c. 67 (UK).

6 On the difficulties in explaining to the Irish just what the Canadian model was, see Lord Longford (Frank Pakenham), *Peace by Ordeal* (London: Sidgwick & Jackson, 1972), p. 200.

7 David Hume, "Idea of a perfect commonwealth," in *Hume: Political Essays* ed. Knud Haakonssen (New York: Cambridge University Press, 1994), p. 222.

8 See Francis Fukuyama, *Political Order and Political Decay: From the Industrial Revolution to the Globalization of Democracy* (New York: Farrar, Straus & Giroux, 2014).

9 Mercatus Center, "The Impossibility of Comprehending, or Even Reading, All Federal Regulations," October 23, 2017.

10 Harvey A. Silverglate, *Three Felonies a Day: How the Feds Target the Innocent* (New York: Encounter Books, 2009).

11 Philip Hamburger, *Is Administrative Law Unlawful?* (Chicago: University of Chicago Press, 2014); Peter J. Wallison, *Judicial Fortitude: The Last Chance to Rein In the Administrative State* (New York: Encounter Books, 2018)

12 Charles M. Tiebout, "A Pure Theory of Local Expenditures," *Journal of Political Economy*, vol. 64, no. 5 (October 1956): 416–24.

13 In *Sáenz v. Roe*, 526 U.S. 489 (1999), the Supreme Court upheld mobility rights by striking down a one-year residency requirement before someone could qualify for state welfare programs. See F.H. Buckley, "Liberal Nationalism," *UCLA Law Review*, vol. 48, no. 2 (December 2000): 221–64.

14 U.S. Bureau of the Census, "Lifetime Mobility in the United States: 2010," American Community Survey Briefs, U.S. Department of Commerce, November 2011.

15 *Gregory v. Ashcroft*, 111 S. Ct. 2395, 2399 (1991). See further Albert Breton, *The Economic Theory of Representative Government* (Chicago: Aldine, 1974), p. 114.

16 Roberta Romano, "Law as a Product: Some Pieces of the Incorporation Puzzle," *Journal of Law, Economics, and Organization*, vol. 1, no. 2 (Fall 1985): 225–83; Roberta Romano, "The State Competition Debate in Corporate Law," *Cardozo Law Review*, vol. 8, no. 4 (March 1987): 709–57.

17 Jørgen Carling, Erlend Paasche and Melissa Siegel, "Finding Connections: The Nexus between Migration and Corruption," *Migration Policy Institute*, May 12, 2015.

18 States might also want to attract the unemployed, for partisan, political reasons. Margaret F. Brinig and F.H. Buckley, "The Market for Deadbeats," *Journal of Legal Studies*, vol. 25, no. 1 (January 1996): 201–32.

19 David S. Law and Mila Versteeg, "The Declining Influence of the United States Constitution," *New York University Law Review*, vol. 87, no. 3 (June 2012): 762–858.

20 Canadian Charter of Rights and Freedoms, s. 1, Constitution Act, S. Can. 1982, enacted as Canada Act, 1982, 31 Eliz. II, c. 11 (UK).

21 Government of Ireland Act, 1920, 10 & 11 Geo. V, c. 67 (UK).

22 *Vriend v. Alberta* , 1 S.C.R. 493 [1998].

23 Alan Wolfe, *One Nation, After All: What Middle-Class Americans Really Think About God, Country, Family, Racism, Welfare, Immigration, Homosexuality, Work, the Right, the Left, and Each Other* (New York: Viking, 1998).

24 Frederick Jackson Turner, *The Frontier in American History* (Mineola, N.Y.: Dover, 1996).

25 Pauline Maier, *American Scripture: Making the Declaration of Independence* (New York: Vintage, 1997). See also Michael Kammen, *A Machine That Would Go of Itself: The Constitution in American Culture* (New York: St. Martin's, 1994); Yael Tamir, *Liberal Nationalism* (Princeton, N.J.: Princeton University Press, 1993).

CHAPTER 12—EVERYTHING THAT RISES MUST CONVERGE

1 Hoover Institution, Golden State Poll, Fieldwork by YouGov, January 5–9, 2017.

2 Henry Adams, *The Education of Henry Adams*, in *Henry Adams: Novels, Mont Saint Michel, The Education* (Library of America, 1983), p. 810.

3 U.S. Bureau of the Census, *Historical Statistics of the United States, Colonial Times to 1970*, Bicentennial Edition, Part 2 (Washington, D.C., 1975), Series Y 308–317, Paid Civilian Employment of the Federal Government: 1816 to 1970, p. 1103. Paul Van Riper would put the number somewhat higher, in *History of the United States Civil Service* (Evanston, Ill.: Row, Peterson, 1958), pp. 57–58. See generally Allen Guelzo, *Abraham Lincoln or the Progressives: Who Was the Real Father of Big Government?* (Washington, D.C.: Heritage Foundation, 2012).

4 See *Governing* Magazine, Data, January 19, 2018; Mike Maciag, "How Much Do States Rely on Federal Funding?" *Governing*, May 22, 2017.

INDEX

North, Frederick North, 8th baron, 120
North Carolina, 28; Research Triangle, 5
North Korea, 82
nullification doctrine, 111–13, 128

Obama, Barack, 5; and Affordable Care Act, 15; and Blagojevich, 77; diktats of, 56; and drug enforcement, 114; and military funding, 83
Obama, Michelle, 11
O'Connor, Flannery, 4
Once and Future King, The (Buckley), 94
Oregon, 20, 125; and ICE, 116
Organization for Economic Cooperation and Development, 64–65
Orwell, George, 91

Paine, Tom, 41
Pakistan, 47
Palin, Sarah, 25
Paris Climate Accords, 19
parliamentary regimes, 83, 93–94
Parnell, Charles Stuart, xi
Parti Québécois, 21, 39–40, 43
Paul, Rand, 10
pay-for-play, 70–71, 75–78, 95
Pearl Harbor attack, 83
Pettigru, James, 5
Philadelphia Evening Journal, 29
Philippines, 47
Piepenbring, Dan, 9
Pierce, Franklin, 37
Pinochet, Augusto, 90
Pledge of Allegiance, 7
Pocock, J.G.A., 78
population, 47–48, 80; of California, 19, 96; density, 64, 65; and happiness, 62–66; and military spending, 84, 87; and social trust, 94–95; and wealth, 99, 107
Posner, Eric, 117
post-contractual opportunism, 104
Putin, Vladimir, x, 10–11, 84–85

Quebec, 3, 21, 104–5; Charter opt-outs, 128; Meech Lake Accords on, 105; opportunism of, 104; secession

referenda in, 25, 39–43; and social welfare, 132; and sovereignty-association, 25, 39, 43, 99

Reconstruction, 6, 7
Reconstruction Amendments, 37
Reference re Secession of Quebec, 39–42
religious faction, 53–54, 72
Republican Party, 15, 56; and heartland, 12
Revolutionary War. See American Revolution
Ripley, William Z., 73
Roberts, John, 70
Roland, Jeanne-Marie, 92
Roman Empire, 51, 81, 86
Rousseau, Jean-Jacques: on federal state, 55; and Hume, 52; on small states, 48, 51–52, 94, 124
Rubin, Jennifer, 106
Ruiz Evans, Marcus, 19, 21
Russia, 64, 66, 107; expansionism of, 84–85; and Finland, 63; Napoleon in, 79, 84; separatism in, 47, 48

Sale, Kirkpatrick, 21
same-sex marriage, 21, 92, 127, 134
Sanders, Bernie, 20
Saudi Arabia, 84
Scarborough, Joe, 10
Schaaf, Libby, 115–16
Schmitt, Carl, 30, 31
Schumer, Chuck, 11
Scotland, ix, 48
Seddon, James, 34
segregation, x, 6, 8, 23–24, 113
Serbia, 129
Sessions, Jeff, 116
Seven Years' War, 41
Seward, William, 33
Sherman, Roger, 52–55, 59, 62, 65
Singapore, 68
Sitwell, Edith, 86
slavery, x, 89–90; and Civil War, 4, 5–6, 29–30, 106; legal protection of, 6, 25, 26, 33
Slovakia, 21, 24
social media, 13, 91–92
Social Security, 126